Steal This Plot

By The Same Authors

The Psychiatric Fix, New York, 1981.
The Private Me, New York, 1980.
How To Live With Other People's Children, New York, 1978.
The Custody Trap, New York, 1975.

Steal This Plot

A Writer's Guide to Story Structure and Plagiarism

by June and William Noble

Paul S. Eriksson

PUBLISHER
MIDDLEBURY, VT. 05753

For D.J.D. with our love

FIRST TRADE PAPERBACK EDITION

Manufactured in the United States of America

10 9 8 7 6 5 4 3

Library of Congress Cataloging in Publication Data -

Noble, June.
    Steal This Plot.

    Bibliography: p.
    Includes index.
    1. Plots (Drama, novel, etc.) 2. Imitation (in literature)
3. Fiction — Technique. I. Noble, William.
II. Title.
P218.N6 1985   808.3   85-6878
ISBN 0-8397-7880-5 (Cloth)
ISBN 0-8397-7881-3 (Paperback)

Contents

Probably almost every conceivable plot has been the subject of many books. However, people will continue to write books, and the public continue to read them, because of the new characters and settings with which the authors surround an old plot, and such of them as are the independent productions of the authors may be copyrighted.

—Goddard, District Judge
Stephans et al v. Howells Sales, Inc. et al, 1926 D.C. New York, 16 F2nd 905.

Preface

This book is *not* about cemeteries.

Nor is it a mystery-suspense story.

It is about writing—the *craft* of writing and telling a tale. It is about how to use other people's stories, and what we are allowed to do with them.

The plot of any story is the key. The plot is the story within the story that propels the action and develops the tale. In *Hamlet*, for instance, the story deals with who will be the rightful king of Denmark, but the plot is concerned with revenge and ambition. The plot is the nucleus of the action, and it is here that the writer must look to form his efforts. *Hamlet* certainly wouldn't be the magnificent drama it is without a plot spilling over with revenge and ambition. The story line moves forward as the elements of the plot slowly unfold: Hamlet's discovery that his uncle murdered his father; Hamlet's killing of Polonius; Laertes' seeking of revenge on Hamlet; the King's scheme to kill Hamlet. These elements of the plot are the basis for the overall story, and without them *Hamlet* becomes a dull tale. The plot keys the story, and that is what this book will demonstrate.

We do not, however, focus exclusively on what some call "great literature." To be sure, we highlight memorable plots from the time of the ancient Greeks to the present day, but a major purpose of this book is to show how a plot in one work can be taken and used in another work—how the plot can be "stolen." For this we don't need to bow in any particular literary direction, so long as we can demonstrate what it takes to steal a plot.

In a police procedural, for example, one might use revenge as a prime story motivator and provide chilling entertainment. In genre fiction—mystery, romance, western, erotic—it is equally possible to use someone else's plot and turn out an exciting tale. The principles for stealing a plot apply across the board with all forms and levels of fiction. The only requirement is a basic understanding of the matrix we've devised: there are a limited number of plots, and they work with a limited number of what we call story spicers. Mix one with the other and a dramatic story line will ensue.

We touch only lightly on other elements of story-making. Characterization, setting, style are crucial, to be sure. But this book is concerned with plot, and if one is seeking a total writing approach, it will not be found here.

Plots are here, though, and in abundance. We start, as Barbara Tuchman does in *The March of Folly*, with the epic story of the Trojan Wooden Horse and its progeny. "The Trojan War," she writes, "has supplied themes to all subsequent literature and art from Euripedes' heart-rending tragedy of *The Trojan Women* to Eugene O'Neill, Jean Giraudoux and the still enthralled writers of our time." We go back to Homer and *The Iliad* and *The Odyssey* for the antecedents to plot-lines that surfaced in Rome at the time of Vergil, again in the medieval period, and then when Chaucer wrote, when Shakespeare wrote, when Goethe wrote....

In short, stealing a plot may be one of the world's oldest professions. The truth is quite clear: almost everyone does it! The main thing we writers must wrestle with is just how much to steal and when does stealing become plagiarizing. When, in other words, does inoffensive larceny become highway robbery!

Not all plots are stolen, of course. In fact, we make no attempt to retrace the origins of some of the plots because it's obvious they originated with the authors. yet even these original plots can show how a story can be molded with a proper motivator. This book is designed to help the writer who seeks to develop a plot. Stealing a plot is one of the ways—but not the only way.

If the value of any technique can be measured by its adherents, then stealing a plot is on the firmest ground. The list is a litany of the familiar: Aristotle... Aristophanes... Terence... Edmund Spenser... John Milton... Samuel Coleridge... Charles Dickens... Henry Wadsworth Longefellow...

In the end, our task may be made easier by the thought that since almost everybody does it, why shouldn't we, too?

PART ONE
Plotting The Steal

1

Structuring The Story

At a writer's conference in New England, an author introduces his audience to his new work of fiction. He relates that the plot is based on an ancient Greek legend — the myth of Daphne, Apollo and Zeus. In essence the author is saying, "I'm going to let you in on a secret. My plot is not new. It comes from somewhere else, and it's thousands of years old."

The author has found his Greek inspiration in Ovid's work — a love poem. Daphne, soft, beautiful and sensuous, bathes in a clear mountain stream. Apollo, by chance or by choice (it doesn't matter), watches her and becomes aroused to the point of abandon. Losing his perspective about courtship and love, he stands up, rampant and ready. Daphne is thrown into near shock and scoots into the woods, Apollo hot on the trail.

At the last moment before the inevitable rape, Zeus, blessed with imagination, turns her into a laurel tree. The still-aroused

Apollo is left with a handful of bark. But laurel twigs whirl into a wreath, and a poet is born, as the crown settles on Apollo's head.

"Now," says the author, "suppose the setting could be changed to the New Hampshire woods, and suppose Daphne is a nubile college girl, and suppose Apollo turns out to be a virile, frustrated local man, and he comes on this latter-day Daphne, not only seductively naked, but *making love* next to the cool waters of a stream?"

She can't turn into a tree. The local man has more sense than to interrupt the love play. So... how about watching?...and stalking? What happens to his ordinary love life? Does he resent the pale, pudgy town girl who has been giving him what he wants for years, who is wordlessly slated to marry him and bear pale, pudgy children for him? Is this the future for him when, within his gaze, is a liberated, rich girl who sparkles from an all-year-round tan acquired at tennis and swimming and other exotic diversions of the privileged?

"As you can see," the author goes on, "I found a plot." Indeed he did! By elementary changes in time, setting, cultural background he was able to map strategy and attitudes to bring everything into a contemporary frame.

The author seems to be challenging his listeners: What could *you* do with this ancient plot idea? Think about it...

The audience's creative wheels start spinning. What if... this plot were set in wartime? What if... the woman were a journalist and the protagonist a villager in a repressive South American country? What if... he intrigues her after frightening her and they become friends... then lovers? What happens to her old boy friend...his old girl friend?

And how about a modern literary reincarnation of the plot? Would F. Scott Fitzgerald's *The Great Gatsby* fit here? After all, Gatsby gazes on the object of his fascination from the safety of his dock. Daisy is "unattainable," "elusive," and uncaring about his feelings. It is amusing to think of his mooning after her. Yet if he became a physical threat, what a change we'd see!

"What if..." is the classic mechanism to take an old story or idea and enhance it with new trappings, to steal a plot and then make it one's own. What if... the time were changed? What if... the locale were changed? What if... the characters had different jobs or different looks or different sets of values?

But let's get back to that writer's conference in New England. At a coffee break after the author has described the Greek plot from which his new novel is taken, the audience reflects on the usefulness of the ancient myth in modern dress:

"So what happens to this modern Apollo? I can't see his just walking away from all this."

"If his modern Daphne doesn't stop romping through these woods in the nude, she'll get zapped by more than acid rain."

A woman interrupts. "I think your remark is stupid and patently sexist. I'm not saying she won't be stalked, but *she*'s not at fault! Look at me. I jog... I hike... and I don't think it's anyone's business. See, you're caught up in the whole bag of woman-as-lure."

"Then why don't you steal the plot and change it your way?"

"Does the young man know this macho back woodsman — this hunk — is a threat? Does his girl friend tell him?"

The woman, again. "What if she doesn't?"

"That could be heavy."

"Good tension and conflict."

"Maybe toying with death."

A man speaks up. "There are options, you know. We haven't even touched on Daphne." He turns to the woman. "Why don't you write it from still another angle?"

"You mean steal the plot, too?"

"Why not?"

If you write a lot, and others know it, you're apt to run into people who will ask: "Where do you get all those ideas?"

A good friend has a special answer for this. He writes fiction periodically for the men's magazines. He produces stories with heavy-breathing fantasy and graphic sexual detail. When someone asks him the usual question about story ideas, they invariably follow it up with: "What does your wife think of what you write?"

He answers, "She thinks I tell a good story. She always asks me, 'Where did you learn that?' "

To preserve domestic harmony, he responds, "I made it up, of course."

Actually, what he "makes up" is two things — a story subject and a story line. He gets the story idea and then he builds on it. One without the other is like an oreo cookie — the inside and the outside taste better when they work together.

So the question about story ideas is really two questions: where do our ideas come from and where do we get the format to carry them along?

Our friend who writes the erotic stories puts it this way: "One day I was on an airplane and happened to sit next to a woman who got to talking about her latest trip to Europe. She was a large woman, single and quite adverturesome. Also, I think she was oversexed. As she began to describe her armorous adventures in some of Europe's capitals, I realized I had the germ of a story. The story idea was simple — an erotic tale of sexual adventure and misadventure in Europe. But I was stuck on what motivation to use for my character's escapades. Then I realized that sexual fulfillment is a motivator. Call it self-discovery, if you like. But it meant that, in itself, the quest for sexual joy is enough to push a story line along. So, "A Nymphomaniac's Tour of Europe" was written and subsequently published in a well-known men's magazine." Then he chuckles. "It was actually anthologized, too."

The chuckle turns into a laugh, "Of course I never saw the woman again, and she never knew she was the model for the story."

Stories are all around us. They're as fresh and available as the air we breathe. Remember the opening lines of that television police drama about New York City some years ago? The announcer intones, "There are eight million stories in the naked city... This is one of them!"

Actually it's a substantial understatement. There are millions upon millions upon millions of stories out there just waiting to be plucked like ripe fruit.

But stories must *do* something. They must go somewhere. It's not enough to say I'll write a story about a man going fishing. He must be going fishing because... or as he is fishing, an event occurs which affects his life... or his fishing is really a metaphor for something else. The story must be affected by some type of situation which moves it ahead.

One of the most popular novels in recent years is Peter Benchley's *Jaws*. Basically it is the story of a huge fish that kills people. But if we stop here, all we have is an idea that sits on itself. Without more it's like chewing air. Benchley's basic story of a man-consuming beast, in fact, has some pretty old roots. In ancient Greece there was the legend of the Minotaur, a beast with the body of a man and the head of a bull, that dwelled on the island of Crete and ate people. But again, without more, the existence of the Minotaur is simply a hideous fact, not a story.

The Greeks, however, were masters at story *telling*, and the legend of the Minotaur soon became interspersed with war and rescue and heroism and treachery. There was now a story line, and a plot.

It went this way. Minos, the ruler of Knossos in Crete, declared war against Athens because he believed his son, Androgeos, was killed by the Athenians. At this time Athens was suffering from a series of afflictions — famine, pestilence, drought — and there was little spirit for a protracted war with Minos. The Athenians consulted their oracle and were told to give Minos whatever he might demand. Some years before, Minos's wife, Pasiphae, had become enamored of a bull, had

had unnatural sexual relations with it and produced the half man, half beast Minotaur. Minos, in his shame and anger, had had the Minotaur, who feasted on human flesh, confined to the Labyrinth, an almost unfathomable maze.

Now against the Athenians, Minos exacted his vengeance. Every ninth year seven young men and seven young women would be provided as fodder for the Minotaur. They would be thrown into the Labyrinth, either to be feasted upon by the Minotaur or to starve to death if they couldn't find their way out.

But when the third round of tribute was due, one of Athens's great heroes, Theseus, offered himself as one of the sacrifices. In reality, of course, he intended to seek out the Minotaur and destroy it. He promised that if he were successful, he would, on the return voyage to Athens, fly white sails rather than the black sails that they had embarked with. And then Athens would be free of the tribute forever.

When he arrived in Crete, Minos's daughter, Ariadne, saw Theseus for the first time and fell in love with him. She decided to help him and gave him a ball of thread with which he could retrace his steps out of the Labyrinth.

The plan worked beautifully. Theseus found the Minotaur asleep, grabbed him by the forelock and killed him. Then, he found his way out of the Labyrinth, was joined by Ariadne and fled Crete.

Now, just as in the Greek legend, Peter Benchley has taken his monster-fish story and sparked it with certain dramatic situations which give it body, substance and — a story line. There's terror and vengeance and heroism as the entire community becomes consumed with the presence of the fish off shore. But all these things are ancillary to the key ingredient at the foundation of the story line — the chase to destroy the monster.

And what is the key ingredient behind the Greek legend of the Minotaur? Theseus's mission to destroy it.

What Benchley has done is to employ a classic device to move a story along. He has taken the story idea and given it motivation. He has used a plot motivator, and this has provided the story line. Now the story has a why and a how.

The chase is but one of the thirteen plot motivators that can be found throughout literature. From the ancient Greek dramas of Aeschylus, Euripedes and Sophocles to the modern prose of Saul Bellow, Ann Beattie and Robert Penn Warren, one or more from a limited list of plot motivators can be found acting to carry each story forward.

Thirteen plot motivators?

Thirteen.

Most of us remember hearing at some point that there really are only 20... or 30... or 40 different ways to tell a story. Or that there are only 16... or 36 different plots ever devised.

The truth is the list can be expanded or contracted on the basis of how general we wish to be. One thing is certain, though: there really is a limited number of basic story lines to follow. Goethe, in fact, said, "It is almost impossible in the present day to find a situation which is thoroughly new. Only the matter of looking at it can be new, and the art of treating it and representing it."

In his reknowned work of more than 60 years ago, Georges Polti came up with 36 dramatic situations which he claimed covered all available story opportunities. Again, depending upon how general or specific we want to become, there really is little room for dispute.

And we should reemphasize that! An attempt to exhaust every possibility is not only a herculean task but an impossible one as well. There really isn't anything new, though we want to be clear about what is basic plot and what is ancillary. For example, when we speak of ambition, one of the thirteen plot motivators, do we also talk of greed? After all, ambition run amuck becomes greed. But is greed really the source for a basic dramatic situation? Is it any more basic than jealousy, arrogance, self-righteousness? Is it as basic to story line as are plot motivators such as ambition, rebellion and catastrophe?

There are certain items which become basic to story construction, and we've chosen to call them "plot motivators." They aren't plots, nor are they dramatic situations. They simply move the plot along and provide drama. There are thirteen in all which cover most available story opportunities for the writer.

But why plot *motivator*?

Because a plot — the story within a story — without some direction is like a large boulder in a bubbling stream. It's a lovely scene. You see it, you might even be able to touch it, *but it doesn't move*! Plot motivators make a story move, and they are the prime devices by which a writer can steal a plot and make it his own.

Take Benchley's *Jaws*. Many have compared it, at least superficially, to Herman Melville's *Moby Dick* in the sense that there is an unremitting chase or search for a great white fish. Here again we have a similar plot — a human-devouring beast that must be destroyed. But look at what Benchley has done. He has asked "what if..." the scene becomes the south shore of Long Island... the fish is a Great White Shark... the hunters are motivated by more financial reward than anything else...

Yet before Benchley's plot will really work, he has to ask why! Why must the fish be destroyed? The answer lies in the plot motivator, i.e. vengeance. Ahab in *Moby Dick* and his counterpart, the fishing boat captain in *Jaws* have both suffered grievous harm from the great white fish, and so they set out to destroy it to salve their own concepts of revenge. Vengeance moves the plot along; it motivates it!

Following are the common plot motivators that appear and reappear through literature. At any given time, of course, more than one plot motivator can exist side by side, affecting the story. The point is that these are the wheels that make the story go; they are the underpinnings for the various dramatic situations. You can take any story idea, attach one or more of these motivators to it, and you'll have a plot and a story line.

In no particular order of importance the plot motivators are:

Vengeance	Persecution
Catastrophe	Self-Sacrifice
Love and Hate	Survival (deliverance)
The Chase	Rivalry
Grief and Loss	Discovery (quest)
Rebellion	Ambition
Betrayal	

As good as plot motivators are in developing a story, there are times when they need further substance and direction. Think, for instance, about Ernest Hemingway's well-told story, *The Old Man and the Sea*. The plot is simple and straightforward: Santiago, an old Cuban fisherman, sets out in his small boat to pursue his livelihood, alone and with just the barest of gear. Far from shore he lands the largest marlin he has ever seen, a fish that if he gets to port intact will rectify, perhaps forever, the misery he has endured throughout his life. Eighty-four days he has gone without catching a fish, and now his salvation is at hand!

Enter the plot motivator — survival. Hemingway paints a vivid portrait of Santiago's fight, not only to land the huge fish but also to get it, intact, back to shore where he would be honored and recognized for such a feat. And it is truly an epic battle for survival, for the fisherman is almost overwhelmed time and time again, first by the huge marlin itself and then by the predators who are drawn to the boat by the trailing blood of the marlin as it remains lashed alongside. So survival is clearly the plot motivator for this story, and a battle for survival is fine story material.

Yet what if the battle for survival was not just a naked struggle but possessed other elements which gave it additional dimension? What if the elements honor and dishonor were add-ed? He *must* land the fish, he *must* bring it in! And with sur-vival as the key plot motivator throughout the story, will it be survival with honor or with dishonor?

What Hemingway had done is to use a plot motivator with something we have chosen to call a "story spicer." It is a device which will add body to an already good story. It will make a plot bolder and more substantial.

Story spicers, in and of themselves, are not strong enough elements to be lumped with plot motivators. They simply can't push a story along by themselves as plot motivators do, yet without them a story line might appear thin.

Are there a limited number of story spicers, just as there are plot motivators?

Here again the answer depends on how general or specific we wish to be. We felt there were thirteen basic plot motivators, and we feel there are thirteen basic story spicers. The great bulk of literature through the ages shows this again and again. But note, this book is not an attempt to be self-limiting or inflexible on the subject of plots; rather, we have extracted well-defined mechanisms that will help in stealing a plot and using it to good purpose.

So if you can find more than thirteen story spicers, use them by all means. Meanwhile, here are the ones we've uncovered:

Deception	Mistaken Identity
Material Well-Being	Unnatural Affection
(Increase or Loss of)	Criminal Action (Including
Authority	Murder)
Making Amends	Suspicion
Conspiracy	Suicide
Rescue	Searching
	Honor and Dishonor

Imagine the following dialogue between a speaker at a writer's conference and his audience of eager listeners:

"There's no problem in stealing a plot. We all do it," the author says.

"Plot motivators are the key. Right?"

The author nods. "You take a story idea, apply a plot motivator, and you have a viable plot. I've shown you how this has been done by every writer since the ancient Greeks."

"I'm still kind of fuzzy," one student says.

"All right," the author says patiently. "Pick a story — something you've read that you liked."

"How about *Catch-22*?"

The author smiles. "Joseph Heller's book."

"Yes."

"Now, we know that the book was essentially a story of one sane man's struggle with the insanity in the military. It had overtones of anti-war, but it was really about the sheer irrationality in the military. Agreed?"

There are nods and murmurs of assent. "Okay, let's play what if..." The author looks at the student. "What if... we pick another institutional setting. Not the military but the..."

"Business world!" the student says.

There is a burst of laughter from the others. But there is general agreement. The author continues. "Now, let's pick a plot motivator, something that will give direction to a story about the sheer irrationality in the business world."

Another student speaks. "In *Catch-22* Yosarian was really just trying to survive. Survival was the main plot motivator."

The author nods. "There may be some who would disagree with you, but I'll concede that was at least *one* of the plot motivators. Okay, pick another for our plot about the business world."

"How about... self-sacrifice?"

More laughter. "That's a pretty rare commodity in the business world," the author says. "But okay. We have a story about irrationality in business where self-sacrifice is the prime motivator. Now, we don't have to follow Heller's style and make this a satire; it can be a serious, well-defined story. A businessman continually bumping heads with the institutional irrationality of the marketplace who sacrifices himself for some broader purpose." The author pauses and looks around. "How about a story spicer?"

The first student speaks up. "Conspiracy," he suggests. "There's a conspiracy which either is directed at the businessman or is one in which he is participating. In either case it dooms him in the end."

The author is grinning now. He pans the room benevolently. "We have a plot with substance and detail. A story about the business community and its strange ways, about a member of that community who, because of sanity amidst irrationality, ends up sacrificing himself for some higher purpose as the victim of a conspiracy. We have a plot, do we not?"

There are nods all around.

"Then," the author smiles, "please use it. We have stolen it, and it is yours."

2

Spicing The Story

Say what you wish about the literary pinnacles achieved by writers such as John O'Hara, Kenneth Roberts, Thomas Costain, Dashiel Hammett, Margaret Mitchell... the appeal of writers such as Rosemary Rogers, Robert Ludlum, Danielle Steele. The literary establishment is prone to scratch its collective head and wonder just what *is* it that makes people want to read such apparently simpleminded stuff.

But the truth is there in plain view: each of these writers, and hundreds of others who have gone before or will come after, mastered the essence of story writing — *they've learned how to tell a good story*! Convoluted circumstances, two- and three-dimensional story lines, lengthy explorations into metaphysical questions may offer the intellectual a comfortable, perhaps an exciting exercise, but for most of us, a good story is a good story is a good story.

What is the writer *saying*? Critics ask this all the time. Clearly, a book that delves into broader areas than simple entertainment is entitled to be judged by standards appropriate to its aims. If the author wishes to explore the sheer obscenity of war and its consequences, as Dalton Trumbo does in *Johnny Got His Gun*, then his book must be held up against others that have tried to do the same thing. Or if an author wants to show how war and revolution can corrupt even the seemingly incorruptible, as Robert Stone does in *A Flag for Sunrise*, then here, also, a measure can be made.

But every story must have a plot, and it is only after creating it that the author can turn attention to working out what it is he or she wants to say. The literary intellectual may choose books that go beyond basic story telling, such as the various works of William Faulkner portraying the decay and decadence of the South, but even so there is story line and plot, too. Sometimes a bit frail perhaps, but without plot and story line all the literary intellectual would be feasting on is a literary essay.

But for a story to be a *good* story, now that's what we're after. Plot motivators will give us the story line, that much is clear. Whether it's a story about vengeance or betrayal or rivalry, or a combination of all three, we come away with the bare construction. We have the framework put together, but there is no paint, no finish, no landscaping.

That's where story spicers come in. They make a story into a good story, they act with plot motivators to give a richness and fullness not otherwise achieved. A story about vengeance is okay, but what if the story is about vengeance achieved through deception? Or what if the story is about ambition, and we spice it with elements of mistaken identity? It doesn't make things more complicated. Just more interesting.

Think of story spicers as road signs that can guide us on a book-writing journey. Using deception, for example, will turn a story in one direction. Using suspicion may turn it in another direction. And keep in mind that combinations of story spicers may also work. In fact, it is a rare book that doesn't have more than one story spicer.

Here, then, are the story spicers that seem to appear and reappear through the literary ages. Some work better with one plot motivator than another, some work better in one genre than another. (For example, suicide would hardly seem appropriate in a light-hearted romance, but it would most certainly be effective in a mystery.) To the author we leave the question of when and where and what and how to apply. . . as we would with any accomplished chef de cuisine.

Deception

The literary antecedents here go all the way back to the legend of the Trojan Horse. "I fear Greeks even when they bring gifts," Vergil wrote in the *Aeneid*, and, of course, he was referring to the deception practiced on Troy by the Greeks with their huge wooden horse. Deception as a literary tool has been common for as long as the written word has been used. The Greek legends abound in stories of deception, as with Prometheus in his quarrel with Zeus over the division of sacrificial meats. Prometheus tries to hide the good meat inside skin and the bones inside fat. Zeus, possibly deceived by the outer wrapping of fat, chooses the bones. The legend then proposes that from this time on, men will always keep for themselves the flesh of sacrificial animals, always offering the fat or inedible parts to the Gods. Zeus, however, is aware of the deception, and in his anger begins to hold the gift of fire from mortals.

Deception is trickery; it's double dealing, fraud and cheating. It doesn't have to spring from dark-hearted motivation; there are deceptions clearly justified, such as the actions of Alec Leamas, the protagonist in John Le Carrés *The Spy Who Came In From the Cold*. For most of the book we see him as a case of spook burnout, and only near the end do we realize he's been deceiving the Russians and playing possum. Deception in the name of honor is efffective as a story spicer but, of course, it doesn't have to be honorable. Heinous actions such as the commission of a crime (blackmail and extortion, even murder fit pretty well here), character assassination, unbridled ambition, greed and lust also work. Deception is a good springboard for rounding off a story; it carries with it the elements of conflict and tension. The reader wonders whether the deception will succeed, how it will succeed, when it will succeed.

Material Wellbeing

Like the plot motivators they work with, story spicers provide movement for a story. They keep things from stagnating. If people are seen either losing or gaining economic worth, the way it happens becomes an important part of the story. As a story spicer, material wellbeing involves both the increase *and* the decrease of the things that make a prosperous life. We say *material* because we want to keep everything fairly narrow. Material wellbeing means an emphasis on things, on creature comforts, as opposed to less tangible effects such as emotional stability. Not that one can't flow naturally from the other, but for purposes of this story spicer we believe the emphasis should be on the physical, on items one can touch.

A classic example of the use of material wellbeing as a story spicer is Margaret Mitchell's *Gone With the Wind*. It is truly an epic of decline and destruction of the South, a harsh splintering of one family's material wellbeing. Two major plot motivators are present here — rebellion and survival — and material wellbeing certainly fits neatly. In fact, whenever the plot motivator is rebellion or survival, the chances are that material wellbeing will be there, somewhere.

Just as material wellbeing can go down, it can also go up. In Jeffrey Archer's novel, *Kane and Abel*, we have the story of two men born on the same day, one to a life of comfort and position, the other to poverty and anonymity. How this latter character rises from such mean circumstances to a life of power and wealth, while carrying on an intense rivalry with someone he has never set eyes on, is the essence of the story. Abel's drive for financial success (translation: material wellbeing) spices up a story hinged on the plot motivator, rivalry. The wealthier Abel becomes, the more power he acquires in his struggle to outdo Kane. The story is immeasurably strengthened in this way.

Authority

Létat c'est moi! stated Louis XIV almost three hundred years ago, and ever since we have had a measure to gauge absolute power. "The state is me," and by that Louis meant that he and he alone was the fountain of all authority. He was the living embodiment of everything French. The authority of France started with him and ended with him.

As a story spicer, authority is an artful technique to establish an immediate conflict situation. Either one bows to authority or one challenges. There really is no middle ground.

Shakespeare plays with the pulls of authority in many of his tragedies. In most cases it is an us-versus-them scenario. Either the characters are behind the authority of the ruler or they are against him. In *King Lear* the king's authority is slowly eroding because of his growing senility. In *MacBeth* the king's authority is challenged because of the ambition of MacBeth. In *Hamlet* the king's authority is challenged because he had killed Hamlet's father, the rightful king. The fact that in each story it is a king who is being challenged makes everything so much more intense and serious. The ultimate authority is the king, and this authority is in danger of toppling.

Authority, of course, can appear in many other circumstances. It can be institutionalized as in the armed services, government, church, school, hospitals; it can be morally based as with a parent or a spouse or any other respected person; it can be physically based through fear or terror or simple intimidation. Authority is the power to command through behavior or thoughts or opinion. A plot which is spiced with elements of authority — whether supported or opposed — provides a concrete story line to follow. Authority is touchable, palpable; we can recognize authority when we see it.

Making Amends

This might be called the guilty-conscience story spicer. We wrong someone, and then we have to decide whether to make it up to them. Do we recompense them, and if so, how?

In Theodore Dreiser's *An American Tragedy*, a young man impregnates a young woman, not out of love but in a moment of lust and passion. Afterwards, he is torn. His true love would be so shocked by what he has done that it would be over between them. Still, he feels something for the other woman, and he is so sorry about what happened. They go out in a small boat in the moonlight, and the young man wants the young woman to try and understand, try to see things from his position. He is so sorry about everything... The young woman goes overboard (helped to an extent by the young man) and is drowned. Eventually the young man is accused and later convicted of murdering her. He wanted to help her. He thought about making amends for getting her pregnant. He tried, he really did.

Sometimes making amends is more successful. In Goethe's *Faust* it takes a lifetime of orgiastic pleasure-seeking for Faust to realize that helping others and providing for their happiness and contentment is the only true source of joy and fulfillment. After taking, taking, taking he finally sees that giving is by far the happier alternative. He makes his amends that way.

Amends-making works best with plot motivators which focus on someone suffering or hurt or otherwise wronged. Betrayal, persecution, vengeance, catastrophe would fall into this category. Of course, the amends-maker need not be the one who did the foul deed. While we may not like it when the sins of the father are visited on the son, human nature is not always so discriminating.

Conspiracy

Two or more people meet, they plot, they plan to do something, they have an end in mind — some definite goal. They *conspire*.

The key is that the entire scheme must result in something wrongful being done. Even if we meet in secret, even if we keep everyone else in the dark, it's not really a conspiracy if what we want to accomplish is perfectly legal and the way we do it is perfectly legal. A conspiracy implies illegality, and that's what makes this story spicer tingle.

Because people doing anything against the law is, in itself, an effective story tool. Conspiracy can be a criminal act, and so it can be linked with criminal action, another story spicer.

But conspiracy doesn't have to be overtly criminal. It can be economically motivated, as with consumers deciding to boycott a certain product or certain business; it can be socially motivated, as with a well-directed snub or shunning.

The great bulk of conspiracy-laden stories, though, are politically motivated. Look at Shakespeare's work: conspiracy after conspiracy in *Othello, Julius Caesar, MacBeth, Richard the Third* — each with some political end. Two or more people get together and they dream of political change, and they act to achieve it. In their actions we see the essential nature of conspiracy; they twist or bend the natural political forces to suit their own ends, they lie, they falsely accuse, they even murder and persecute. The way conspiracy operates, the wrongful aims and the wrongful ends are the necessary ingredients for building tension and conflict. Imagine *Julius Caesar*, for example, if Brutus had decided to kill Caesar on his own, without being urged by Cassius or anyone else. Brutus's reasons might have been just as sound, but the entire nature of the story would have been changed. Brutus would stand out as a lone assassin and not as personifying the groundswell of public objection to Caesar's ambition. Could Brutus be so sympathetic under these circumstances? Could his character be so evened-off as it is by contrast with the motivations of the other conspirators?

The modern political novel is replete with conspiracy and counter-conspiracy. We need only read Robert Ludlum (*The Holcroft Covenant*, for example) or Steve Shagan (*The Circle*) to see how effective conspiracy can be at spicing up a story. Take any plot motivator, sprinkle a dash of conspiracy and — voilá! A story line.

Rescue

Most commonly, this story spicer can be found when the plot involves physical danger or peril. Will he/she make it? Will the rescue work? Plot motivators such as catastrophe, persecution, survival are natural tie-ins with rescue because each can be founded on some element of physical danger. Is there ever a catastrophe without physical danger? When persecution is in the air, isn't there danger all around? When we survive some traumatic event, aren't we rescued?

Typical of this kind of story is Hammond Innes's *The Land God Gave to Cain*, published in 1958. The action takes place in Labrador following an eerie radio message received by a ham operator in London. The message is sent by a man supposedly killed in an airplane crash, and it begins a tale of search and rescue that slogs its way through unbelievably rugged wilderness which compounds the constant physical danger. It is a story of survival with the hope of rescue spurring the characters on.

In most stories involving rescue, the presence of another story spicer — searching — can be found. To rescue someone or something, there first has to be a search. Then comes the rescue. Even where the rescue consumes the story almost in its entirety, a search for some type of final absolution or honor will generally occur. In Walker Percey's fine novel, *The Second Coming*, for instance, the rescue of a schizophrenic girl from her mental strait jacket consumes much of the book, but as the protagonist performs his rescue, he also searches for some divine order in the events as they unfold. The search is there as the rescue takes place. And the rescue, of course, is not so much from physical danger as from emotional turmoil. Danger is no less severe when it is directed in the mind, and a rescue from that kind of circumstance is no less intriguing as a story spicer.

Mistaken Identity

It started with the gods and goddesses in the earliest Greek legends. Zeus and Hera and Apollo and Athena and Aphrodite — all would assume mortal roles for some specific purpose, and then, after they had accomplished their goal, they would return to being gods and goddesses. In the *Odyssey*, Homer writes: "Owl-eyed goddess Athena smiled at (Odysseus's) words and stroked him with her hand; she was in the likeness of a woman fair and tall and accomplished in glorious works, and she spoke winged words to him. . ."

Or Apollo, taking the shape of a dolphin in *The Hymn to Apollo*, jumps aboard a ship from Crete and diverts it to the bay of Crisa where he finally reveals himself and demands that those around him build a temple in his honor. "I declare to you that I am the son of Zeus; I am Apollo" he says. "I brought you here over the great gulf of the sea with no evil intent, but you shall possess here my rich temple held in much honor among all men, and shall know the counsels of the immortals and by their help be continually honored for all your days. . ." Thus the Delphic Oracle is born.

Adventure stories seem a natural home for plots which are spiced with mistaken identity. Stories of vengeance, for example, where one of the prime characters is not who the others think he is. Or stories of love and hate where mistaken identity has precipitated such deep feelings. Or stories of a rivalry which might never have existed if there hadn't been a misstep about who was who. In Daphne du Maurier's *The Scapegoat* an Englishman meets a Frenchman by chance in a railroad station in Le Mans. They bear an amazing likeness to one another, and the Englishman is forced to assume the Frenchman's identity and move into his household where he is surrounded by hate and suspicion and rivalry. Mistaken identity is the story spicer that moves this plot along because the Englishman has no choice but to play his role, and the remainder of the household continue in ignorance as the entire story unfolds.

Mistaken identity works from two directions: we see it from the point of view of the one assuming the wrong identity or from the aspect of those relying on the wrong identity. Either way we have a built-in story advantage: will anyone discover the mistaken identity? How will he/she continue to cover up the mistaken identity? What happens when the mistaken identity is revealed?

Unnatural Affection

The Greek legends abound with this type of spicer. From Zeus transforming himself into a bull in order to make love to Danae, the mother of Perseus, to the act of love performed between Pasiphae, wife of Minos, King of Crete, and a bull to the passion of Phaedra, wife of Theseus, for her stepson, Hippolytus (which is further dramatized by Euripedes in his play, *Hippolytus*)... to the incest between Oedipus and his mother, Jocasta (also further dramatized by Sophocles in his *Oedipus Tyrranus*).

The point is that any form of passion, whether physical, emotional or both, that steps out of the normal man-woman, adult-adult, non-blood-related framework has a claim to be called "unnatural," and this surely creates an intriguing story line. It's different, it's unusual, it's interesting. John Irving could have a brother and sister in wild bouts of passion in *Hotel New Hampshire*, and lend a wacky tilt to a story about a family who runs a hotel. Survival, perhaps even discovery, may have been the prime plot motivators, but doesn't it add an air of intrigue and sheer anti-establishment nose thumbing to have a running account of incest?

Of course the ultimate question of what is "natural" and what isn't depends on the lean of the observer. Is homosexuality or lesbianism or even transvestitism natural? To some they are, though it's safe to say that the large majority might not think so.

Yet a work of fiction where homosexuality (see, for example, E.M. Forster's *Maurice*) or lesbianism (see, for example, Marge Piercy's *Small Changes*) plays an important part might shower the reader with aspects of unnatural affection and carry a fairly conventional story line. In Thomas Mann's *Death in Venice*, we have a story of a reknowned author on vacation who gradually falls in love with a young Polish boy, his feelings ultimately consuming him so that he even ignores the threat of an impending cholera epidemic. Survival, discovery, and love and hate are the major plot motivators, and if we erase the unnatural affection, we have a conventional story line without much passion. But when we add pederasty to the mix, things become not so conventional, then!

Criminal Action

Any act against the law makes a good story. The conflict is built in, the black hats against the white hats. And it doesn't matter from which side one writes the story or which plot motivator we use. They all work here. We sympathize with the bouts of conscience Macbeth suffers even though we know him to be a murderer and a political outlaw. We applaud the unselfishness and higher motives of Brutus even as we read about his plunging his dagger into Caesar's body. On the other hand we find it easy to identify with those intrepid characters who hunt down the criminals — private eyes, police detectives, federal-government spooks — and while genre fiction on this side of the law-enforcement ledger appears to have a monopoly, let's not forget one crucial fact above all — it's a *good* story we're really after, and we have to be good story tellers! Genre fiction or no, criminal action spices up a story.

Murder, treason, larceny, rape, assassination, extortion,

blackmail, counterfeiting, arson — these and many more are the types of events that add body to a story. Imagine a Shakespearean tragedy without at least one murder. Or any of the great adventure novels such as Jules Verne's *Twenty Thousand Leagues Under the Sea*; or Charles Nordhoff's *Mutiny on the Bounty*; or a great political novel such as Robert Penn Warren's *All the King's Men* — without a criminal act taking place. The plot motivators may hinge on ambition or vengeance or self-sacrifice or survival, but when someone plans or commits a criminal act in the course of the story, it means so much more in terms of characterization, plot direction and ultimate story resolution.

Look at it this way. What if. . . an upstanding citizen of a major city is quietly arrested for shoplifting. There's no police record and no medical record of emotional instability. The shoplifter is successful in business, has a fine, attractive family, is well respected within the community and offers no reason for the crime. Is this not an intriguing plot concept? Would it be less intriguing if there had been no shoplifting? Does it matter which side this story is written from? Don't we want to know *why*?

You bet we do.

Suspicion

This story spicer occurs in the minds of the characters rather than as an overt event. If we suspect someone of doing or not doing something, the process by which we get there is based on things happening that move us into an area of distrust. Distrust. That's the bottom line with suspicion. If we suspect someone, we distrust them, and if we distrust them, we have a natural conflict to work with.

Obviously, suspicion is always present with the police procedurals, the detective stories, the suspense genre. Suspicion — or distrust — is what makes this type of book go because it sets up (as with criminal action) the good guys-bad guys format.

Yet suspicion is really a preliminary step to criminal action. It's in the head, a surmise, a guess, but in no way does it confirm that something criminal or against the law has taken place. And that's why it has its intellectual side. Is the suspicion justified, we can ask. What *actually* has happened to create the suspicion, and are we seeing those events in their proper perspective? What's the motive for the suspicion? Perhaps the one doing the suspecting is the one we should suspect. There are many variables with suspicion, many levels and approaches we can take. For example, in Daphne du Maurier's *Rebecca*, suspicions abound over just who Rebecca was, what happened to her and why. The story moves from one ominous circumstance to another, leaving behind a growing pile of suspicions with little resolution until the end. Distrust is palpable throughout the book, even though the plot motivator fluctuates between survival and love and hate. Suspicion is what really gives it substance.

For the most part suspicion works best with motivators like betrayal, vengeance, rivalry, survival, rebellion and persecution. That's because these plot motivators demand strong conflict situations, and suspicion is in itself a conflict-laden condition. If we suspect someone of something, we sure don't want to make ourselves vulnerable, do we?

So we step back, button ourselves up and watch our suspicions grow and grow.

Suicide

This is a corollary to the story spicer, criminal action. When we commit a crime, we are doing something unlawful to someone else; when we commit or try to commit suicide, we are doing the same thing to ourselves. (Actually, attempting to commit suicide is, in itself, a crime and a violation of most state statutes. But the law is rarely enforced in this connection.)

The idea of suicide comes in many forms: as a political statement, as the ultimate despair in a failed love affair, as the only release from degradation and horror, as a form of penance, as a compulsive pursuit of unlimited earthly pleasures. Motivations are as varied as the ways we set about killing ourselves, but one thing is clear: the act of suicide conjures up an unsettling barrage of questions. How can someone do that to themself! What's the *real* reason! Did he/she have to go *that* far?

It seems to us that the truth of suicide is this: it's embarrassing to family and friends; it's a final clutch at some form of reality; it's rarely without pain; it's an extremely self-centered act; it's the ultimate rebellion.

It's also a fine technique for spicing up a story, and it works best with plot motivators that can strip a story line to its raw, emotional edge, such as catastrophe, grief and loss, love and hate, persecution, betrayal. Suicide is a catastrophic event, and the feelings it engenders can be equally as substantial.

Suicide, of course, doesn't have to be a single, lone event, happening without warning. There can also be a process to suicide, a slow disintegration that culminates in death. In Gustave Flaubert's *Madame Bovary*, we see moral degeneration taking place, one step after the other, a slow sinking into despair, the result of trying to survive the sheer boredom of provincial life. Joan Didion in *Play It As It Lays* also picks up the theme of a character in the midst of an arid life. In this case Didion has her character indulging herself with pills, drugs, sexual experimentation — anything, in fact, to numb her to the pain of living. Survival is the plot motivator in both these works, but suicide is what is happening. Survival, in fact, fights a losing battle.

Searching

Most often this story spicer should be used in conjunction with rescue. If we search, we hope to find. And if we find, the chances are we're going to be doing some rescuing. Searching implies that something or someone is lost or must be found. Note the difference, though: just because we find something doesn't mean it's been "lost." Some people — such as the waterclerk in Joseph Conrad's *Lord Jim* — don't want to be found. So when we search, it may not be for someone or something that's been lost. Just missing would be better.

Searching works well with plot motivators such as discovery, survival and the chase. Story lines that move the action quite a bit seem natural here because a search implies a series of events that carries us in one direction or another. Of course, we can search not only for someone or something, but for ourselves. That is, we can hope to discover who we are when set against events that are destined to test us. It is one of Hemingway's favorite themes, one he propounds in a variety of works, from Jake Barnes in *A Farewell to Arms* to Robert Jordan in *For Whom the Bell Tolls*. We face a series of tests, and they turn us into a better, stronger human being or they don't. We come to know ourselves and to discover what we can and can't do.

Searching for ourselves or for someone or something else, has strong antecedents in Homer's *Odyssey* and *Iliad*. The journey of Odysseus after the fall of Troy is the picture of a massive search, set against a backdrop of survival and discovery. The Lotus-eaters, Polyphemus the Cyclops, Aeolus, king of the winds, the huge Laestrygonians, Circe, Scylla and Charybdis, the cattle of the Sun, Calypso's island — these and more are the tests for Odysseus as he makes his way home in the years following the Trojan War. Odysseus is searching for home and in the process he finds himself.

Honor and Dishonor

This is perhaps the simplest and easiest of the story spicers to use. It works with every plot motivator because it deals with human nature and its changeable form. In a story of betrayal, for example, how the characters act with one another could be hinged on how they honor one another; in a story of grief and loss, is there honor in the aftermath of the mourning? In a story of self-sacrifice, is there dishonor in the ultimate demise?

Honor and dishonor have reference to esteem, both public

and private. If we have a sense of honor, it's generally because we have a feeling of self-esteem. We respect ourselves, and thus we can share that respect in our feelings for others. We honor ourselves as we honor others. And the world honors us in return.

Take *Julius Caesar*. Brutus tells Cassius as they converse about Caesar's worrisome ambition that honor is something he holds higher than almost anything else. "For let the gods so speed me as I love the name of honour more than I fear death," Brutus says. And Cassius responds, "I know that virtue to be in you, Brutus...."

It is a story of honor even in the commission of a crime. Brutus remains an honorable man. He is driven to kill Caesar *because* he is an honorable man. He looks for nothing for himself, no rewards of any kind. At the funeral orations, Mark Antony calls Brutus an "honorable man" over and over, implying, of course, just the opposite. But regardless of how the reader ultimately feels, the point is that honor and dishonor have been used as a means to add depth to the story. Suppose, for example, Brutus is not so honorable. What kind of story would there be? Little sympathy for the conspirators, much more identification with Caesar... and probably a much less well-balanced drama. It is in Brutus's sense of honor that we see Caesar and his ambition unveiled, for if such an honorable man as Brutus is moved to kill, perhaps Caesar deserved such a fate.

The story line may have been founded on ambition, but it is in the clash between concepts of honor and dishonor that substance and spice have been added. Honor and dishonor... public and private esteem... it's how we feel about ourselves and about others that turns the trick.

PART TWO
Motivating The Plot

3

Vengeance

"Vengeance is mine, I will repay!" said The Lord.

Vengeance, than man-eating shark of an emotion, tears at the innards while it propels the protagonist into action. The urge for vengeance is obsessive. To write about it properly, one must portray it as consuming, all-encompassing. Vengeance *is* an obsession. That is the primary thing to remember.

We have been told that long-standing Greek custom requires a man to avenge the murder of his brother. Until he does, the dead brother will not rest quietly. He may cause havoc from the grave. Even a mild, self-effacing victim could turn into a demon if the crime against him is not avenged. The surviving brother or brothers are duty bound to seek vengeance.

The plot motivation is clear: the brother seeks the killer, finds him and does away with him. Peace reigns.

But look how an accomplished writer molds and fits this plot motivator for the contemporary scene. Harry Mark Petrakis, whose work has been nominated for the National Book Award, explores the issue in his novel, *Days of Vengeance*. He considers these questions: what if. . . the setting for the opening scenes is rural Greece in the first decade of the twentieth century; and what if. . . the victim is slated to go to America to join his uncle; and what if. . . he is a kind and trusting young man, and before he emigrates he is killed by a pathologically envious contemporary; and what if. . . the brother emigrates in the victim's place; and what if. . . the killer emigrates to America as well?

Vengeance is clearly the plot motivator in this story, but something more is needed to give fullness to the tale. So Petrakis adds a story spicer — the search. The story moves from Greece to Ellis Island to Chicago to the bestial labor camps at the mines and railroads in the western United States. It revolves about the obsession for vengeance while the avenger searches for his victim across the face of the continent. The story line is a neat mixture of plot motivation — vengeance — and story spicer — searching.

In Euripedes' *Medea* vengeance is the concept of the scorned woman. Medea had been left by Jason for another woman, and in her fury Medea poisons her rival and then kills the children she had borne with Jason. Story spicers in this ancient tale include honor and dishonor and the commission of crimes — specifically, murder. But the motivation for the story, the track that the story moves upon, is vengeance. Medea wants revenge; why she wants it and how she gets it are ancillary to the essence of the story.

Shakespeare deals with vengeance in a number of his works, but in *The Tempest* it is quite clearly the prime plot motivator. What if. . . one brother, Antonio, drives another brother, Prospero, into exile and usurps the family throne; and what if. . . Prospero lands on a barely inhabited island in the South Atlantic and is somehow blessed with magical powers; and what if. . .

these magic powers cause Antonio to become shipwrecked on the island and to come within the control of Prospero? How the vengeance is wrought and what other discomforts are experienced by Antonio and his family liven up the basic story, but it is Prospero's urge for vengeance that carries things along.

Vengeance, standing alone, can be an extremely powerful thrust to any story. But when it combines with another plot motivator, is its effect diluted or enhanced? In Sidney Sheldon's work, *Master of the Game*, for instance, we have vengeance *and* ambition. The plot begins in a straightforward manner. A dissatisfied Scot, Ian McGregor, tired of being poor and bored, nurses the idea that there could be riches for him if he could find the right slot. Letters and twice-told tales from Africa encourage this. Since McGregor is fit and young, and youth goes where others fear to walk, it is the diamond mines in South Africa that grab his attention. His vision is so strong that he can put up with the disgusting voyage, fatal to many. After being gulled and brutally attacked to the point of death by a hypocritical Dutchman he is befriended by a black man, one of a band that had been ordered to do him in.

His conversion from trusting greenhorn to worldly-wise entrepreneur is complete when he collects enough diamonds and becomes rich and powerful enough to break his enemy, the Dutchman. He reduces him to poverty and shame.

Vengeance to the point of psychosis does not end with McGregor. It is passed on to his daughter, Kate. As she grows, there is only one man she wants — a friend of her father's. He teaches her how to be master of the big game, the world of business and finance, and she is a willing student. She manipulates her power to get exactly what she wants. Her view of the world is skewed, and she requires careful watching. Yet who could imagine the methods she would use to arrive at her own ends? She can move people as chess pieces, buy what she wants, scheme and plot to achieve her aims.

Sheldon tries to humanize her, showing a ''good'' side. She is concerned about white-black relationships in Africa, and there are some scenes showing her sensitive side to bear this out. She also is considered a soft touch for funds for endangered Jews during World War II. These redeeming portions of her character are shallow and contrived, however. The good she could be accomplishing is far overshadowed by her singleness of purpose to get what she wants.

She is assumed to be bright with innate intelligence. It is hard to spot. She simply gets what money will buy. In fact, she is practically simpleminded about her granddaughters. Twins, one is the personification of evil, the other of trusting goodness. Kate, though, can't see beyond her nose.

Is this a book we might like to read? The African setting is unusual, Kate is perhaps no worse than other diabolical women, and the plot moves ahead with speed. Yet the good Kate could do is pushed aside by her emotionless manipulation, starting with trapping a husband and continuing through the wrecking of her son's career. With greed and ambition as the driving motivators, she tears down her friends, her son and potentially her young granddaughters.

Has Sheldon applied story spicers? What about deception? The theiving Dutchman is his first instrument of deception and naturally this then fuels other deceptions as McGregor, returning with his fortune and bristling with revenge, pulls the old man's world down, and his daughter's reputation, as well.

Note how misunderstandings can keep a plot jumping. The reader, in frustration, may yell to the characters, ''Talk it out, you are misreading this.'' But just as soap operas have thrived on unresolved misunderstandings, so do many good books. Tension flows from this type of thing.

See how Sheldon uses misunderstanding, blending it with the undercurrent of vengeance. The self-righteous Bible-thumping Dutchman is, himself, a child-molester. His black employee, who had saved McGregor's life, lost a twelve-year-old sister. She died giving birth to the child forced on her by the Dutchman's rape. McGregor knows that nothing is more important to the Dutchman than the virginity of his own daughter, and when she ends up with McGregor's child, he tosses her to the town and pushes it in the Dutchman's face. He assumes the daughter is equally as guilty as the Dutchman for stealing his goods and almost costing him his life. She isn't, of course, but a misunderstanding like this keeps the plot moving.

Can a multi-national business flourish with open and above-board tactics? Not in Sidney Sheldon's literary world. Conspiracy is handmaiden to McGregor and his daughter, and Kate realizes its powerful use from her teens onward. She has been taught to be the best. And so she becomes a master without scruples who has little to offer anyone except a seat next to power and a well-groomed face. In place of warmth there is authority, joining deception as a story spicer. If we know this about a character, isn't it inevitable that the story can move and flow? How does Kate handle a daughter-in-law? Is her value as a person only in how her offspring performs? If progeny means so much, to what lengths would Kate go to encourage a life-threatening pregnancy? If she wants her son to rule the diamond world with her, to what lengths would she go to squash his artistic career?

Can we imagine the sport of the author, casting to find intricate ways to manipulate her diabolic mind? Vengeance backed-by ambition is a most powerful plot motivator, indeed.

"Revenge is a kind of wild justice which the more man's nature runs to, the more ought law to weed it out." Francis Bacon made this observation several centuries ago, and it's an apt expression about the pervasive disharmony that accompanies the urge for vengeance. It results in powerful emotions and forceful actions because it implies an ultimate payback.

And no clearer example can be uncovered than in the work

that many consider the model for revenge-seeking in the annals of literature: Aeschylus's *Oresteia* or *The House of Atrius*. Called a revenge trilogy by critics, *Oresteia* consists of three dramas that begin with the start of the Trojan War and with the murder of the war hero, Agamemnon, by his wife, Clytemnestra. The trilogy ends with the murder of Clytemnestra by her son, Orestes, and his subsequent persecution by his mother's ghost and the Furies until he receives final absolution through the Gods.

Though we'll explore this work in greater detail in Chapter Nine (Betrayal), it offers a good example for our purposes here as to how revenge-seeking carries with it the seeds of its own perpetuation, crime begetting crime with no seeming end. Agamemnon, on his way to the Trojan War, sacrifices his daughter, Iphigenia, which brings his wife, Clytemnestra, to hate him. She kills him with the help of her lover, Aegisthus. (*His* father, Thyestes, had been forced to eat the flesh of his own children by Agamemnon's father, Atrius.) Orestes kills Clytemnestra and Aegisthus to avenge his father, Agamemnon. The Furies then persecute Orestes.

The Greeks were well aware that a tale founded on revenge brought out a strong story line, one with which people could identify and take sides. It allows the writer to develop a variety of themes such as the arrogance of power, the retrieval of honor, the urge for wealth and position, the righteousness of simple justice. All of these (and more) are explored in *The House of Atrius*, and none could have achieved such fine portrayal except within the clamor and the wrench of vengeance sought and vengeance done.

It is plot motivation on a grand scale because Aeschylus deals with universal themes of love and hate, life and death and man's essential subjugation to a higher will. Vengeance is *not* without its cost. No mortal is immune from the ultimate payback.

Some twenty-five hundred years later, the same panorama of values and judgments, obsessions and satisfactions are displayed on an equally grand scale in Herman Melville's classic, *Moby Dick*. Here we have vengeance sought not against a human, but against a white whale, and the struggle is a testament to man's urge to erase a lifelong scar that pulses with his own fallibility. If... the whale could be destroyed, that would underscore the righteousness of the vengeance. If... man could exact his revenge *and* survive, that would be a testament to his essential superiority over non-human beings.

The plot, which carries many of the same themes that Aeschylus uses in *The House of Atrius*, concerns the whaling voyage of the ship, *Pequod*, out of Nantucket. Ishmael, a schoolmaster with a yen for sea travel, signs on and becomes friendly with a tatooed harpooner, Queequeg. The ship is enroute to the Indian Ocean in the hunt for whales, and the first few days of the voyage are fairly calm as the ship is handled by the first mate, Starbuck. Captain Ahab, the skipper, is nowhere to be seen, but after a time, he appears on deck, a rigid man with a dour expression and a white scar running from his cheekbone right down to and under his collar. He has only one leg, the other just a stump supported by the bone from the jaw of a whale. It is soon evident that his obsession to find and kill the white whale is total, and after a few days, he calls the men to him at the foot of the mainmast. In solemn ceremony Ahab takes a gold piece and nails it to the mast, promising that the first sailor to sight the white whale will get it. Then, he orders liquor broken out so that each member of the crew may have a cup. Drink! he orders. Drink to the death and the destruction of Moby Dick!

Over the next few months the *Pequod* continues south around the Cape of Good Hope, having a fair run of luck but never sighting Moby Dick. Queequeg, the harpooner, has demonstrated his skills in the various whale kills, and he and

Ishmael have become close friends. Whenever the *Pequod* encounters another whaling vessel, Ahab asks for news of the white whale but no one has anything to offer. (Note how Melville uses foreshadowing by allusions to the white whale, especially when one sea captain warns Ahab not to try and destroy Moby Dick. The menace of the white whale grows stronger with every reference.)

Then the *Pequod* enters the Indian Ocean, and encounters an English whaler. "Have you news of the white whale?" Ahab asks. For an answer, the captain of the English ship holds up his arm and shows nothing from the elbow down but a sperm-whale bone. They have met Moby Dick and have lived to tell of it! This is what Ahab has been waiting for. But the other captain urges him to reconsider. It would be foolhardy to try and track the white whale. It is much too dangerous.

But Ahab is a man possessed. He finds out where the English captain encountered Moby Dick, and sets sail for the white whale's new feeding ground.

In the meantime Queequeg has become sick and feverish. He asks the ship's carpenter to make him a coffin shaped like a canoe because he is certain he will die, and he wishes familiar comfort for his final journey. The coffin is placed in Queequeg's cabin, but instead of dying, he is restored to health. He then spends his quiet hours carving exotic designs all over the coffin.

And the search for the white whale continues. Ahab challenges the elements and the fury of God in his pursuit of Moby Dick, urging his men to ignore their fear and concern. If we kill the white whale we will find our own salvation, he tells them.

Then the white whale is sighted, and it is Ahab himself who spots him first. Finally he will have his revenge.

Or will he? The first day Ahab takes command of the lead whaleboat in pursuit of Moby Dick, and just as he gets close enough to hurl the first harpoon, the whale suddenly turns about, dives under Ahab's boat and splinters it, throwing Ahab and his men into the sea. Then Moby Dick slides away into the depths, while the other whaleboats pick up Ahab and his men. Once aboard the *Pequod* again, the Captain's obsession is charged to new heights. First blood in the final contest has been drawn, and it is a tonic to his vengeance-seeking. Ahab strides to the mainmast with the gold doubloon still nailed there:

Men, (he says), this gold is mine, for I earned it; but I shall let it abide here till the White Whale is dead; and then, whosoever of ye first raises him, upon the day he shall be killed, this gold is that man's; and if on that day I shall again raise him, then ten times its sum shall be divided among all of ye!

On the second day the *Pequod* once more catches up with Moby Dick. The whaleboats are lowered, and this time three harpoons find their mark. But the whale begins churning and twisting in such fashion that the harpoon lines are crossed and gnarled. The boats are thrown in different directions and finally splintered. Then, once more, Ahab's boat is attacked by the whale, and this time Ahab is lifted out of the water and thrown skyward and into the sea, while the white whale sounds and escapes. As before, Ahab and his men are picked up and returned to the *Pequod*.

Then comes the third day and the climax of the story. Still burning with his need for vengeance, Ahab once more is able to find the white whale, now trailing the harpoons and the lines that found their mark the day before. The boats are lowered for the confrontation, but this time the white whale is enraged as never before, and he turns on the boats before they have a chance to do him deadly harm. On the *Pequod* the mate, Starbuck, believes everyone is in mortal danger and so turns the ship towards the whale in order to save what is left of the crew. But Moby Dick swims straight at the *Pequod* and smashes it in collision. Ahab, still afloat in his boat, now hurls his harpoon into the side of the whale. But he doesn't realize that the rope-coils on the harpoon are around his neck, and as the harpoon digs itself into the whale's flank, the line plays out and suddenly Ahab is pulled from his boat into the sea.

In the end, the only one to survive is Ishmael, and he does so by clinging to the strangely designed coffin once made for his friend, Queequeg. The vengeance Ahab sought with such passion comes to nothing. It is the same message Aeschylus sends out in *The House of Atrius* — only the Gods can exact vengeance. A mere mortal attempts it at his ultimate peril.

"Vengeance is mine..." said The Lord.

So it is.

4

Catastrophe

There's a story that goes this way...

One day two old friends meet on the street. They haven't seen one another for some time. "And how is that new business you were going to buy into the last time we talked?" the first one asks.

"We went bankrupt two months ago. Most of my money is gone."

"How terrible! It must be very painful for you."

"It is, it is."

"And how is your joyful little daughter?"

The second man shakes his head. "She was hit by a car last month. Dead on arrival at the hospital."

"Oh!" the first man gasps. "A tragedy! Such a tragedy! You and your wife must be suffering greatly."

"My wife died two weeks ago of a heart attack."

"A catastrophe, that's what you've lived through! A catastrophe!"

"Ah," says the second man, the edges of a smile on his lips, "but you haven't heard the good part yet..." at which point lightning strikes him, and he falls to the street, dead.

Catastrophe... a series of calamities or disasters that end in supreme despair or ruin. Catastrophe — a situation filled with various misfortunes that, taken together, amount to destruction.

Catastrophe as a plot motivator is a surging force on a story, a most powerful influence. Catastrophe, by its very nature, carries along the elements of good story making — tension, of course, high drama, essential conflict, life-and-death struggles. It really isn't hard to understand the impact of catastrophe on story line.

Through the ages writers have used catastrophe to move their plots along. Homer, in *The Iliad* and *The Odyssey*, uses it over and over. In fact, in the opening book of *The Iliad*, he writes of a pestilence that has invaded the camp of the Greeks who have been beseiging Troy for almost ten years. It seems that Chryses, Apollo's priest, wants to gain his daughter back from Agamemnon, Commander of the Greek armies. Agamemnon has been using her as a concubine, and he doesn't want to give her up. So Chryses prays to Apollo for intervention, and Apollo responds by sending a pestilence. In *The Odyssey* Homer writes of shipwrecks, of life-and-death struggles with the one-eyed Cyclops, of having a ship's crew changed into swine, of a descent into Hades and the battles with Scylla and Charybdis — events which border on catastrophe because Odysseus, the protagonist, survives by just the barest margin. Catastrophe as a plot motivator is effective even if it doesn't occur, so long as the threat of its happening is there and the consequences seem very real and frightening.

Catastrophe, actually, comes in several shapes, and as a plot motivator its shape ultimately determines the story line. For example, the most common type of catastrophe is of the natural variety — earthquake, flood, famine, drought and the like. We build a story on the foundations of a natural catastrophe, as Albert Camus did with *The Plague* in 1947. This story is set in Oran, Algiers in the 1940s, and the leading character is Bernard Rieux, a young doctor. For several days Rieux finds rat bodies on the landing of the stairs to his apartment each morning. The rats have died from internal bleeding, and the concierge grumbles about having to clean them up. Day by day the number of rat bodies increases, and soon truckloads are being carted away. Then the concierge comes down with a fever and Rieux treats him for it and for painful swellings. Rieux calls some of his colleagues around Oran and finds that they, too, have had such cases.

The head prefect is notified, but he doesn't want to take any strong action because of his fear that the local population might be unduly alarmed. He cautions patience, even though one doctor makes it plain to him that he thinks the city is afflicted by bubonic plague. But people begin dying, and shortly the death toll rises to thirty a day. The prefect is then implored to do something drastic... but still the death toll climbs. In the local papers, the weekly count of deaths has become a daily count. Armed guards are set up at all the entrances and exits to and from the city, allowing no one to enter or leave. Citizens are forbidden to send or receive mail, and the telephone lines become so heavily overburdened that the only reliable way of communicating with the outside world is by telegraph. Body disposal becomes a problem, and the authorities begin to cremate the remains in older graves to make room for the new bodies. Two pits are dug in a field, one pit for women, one pit for men. But even these pits become filled, so still another, larger pit is dug and this time there is no attempt to segregate the sexes. Men, women and children are simply thrown into the larger pit and covered with a layer of quicklime. Rieux works in a ward at the infirmary, but there is little he can do to stem the onslaught of the disease. The available serum is ineffective, and most of the patients die. All Rieux can do is try to make their hours and days a bit more comfortable.

Camus weaves various characters through the story, interpreting their reactions to the plague as a commentary on good and evil, God and man, retribution and penance, the fulfillment of one's life. These heady themes all play through the book while Camus works his plot along, grinding the horrendous conditions ever more severe.

And finally, with the coming of cold weather in the middle of winter, the plague dies away. But, of course, the lives of those it affected will never be the same.

Can we steal Camus' plot? It doesn't have to be a plague, or even a natural catastrophe. It can be any momentous event which throws people into situations where they can be manipulated by the author into professing views or taking action on the grander questions of our time. A volcanic eruption, perhaps? Or an out-of-control forest fire? What about the slowly disintegrating layer of ozone in our atmosphere which protects us from the scorching rays of the sun? What if... we take Camus' Doctor Rieux and make him a coal miner caught in a huge underground explosion with many others? Or a meteorologist in the center of a massive tornado scourge? Or a ship's captain threatened by a massive hurricane? The actions of the characters are conditioned by the catastrophe, and the movement of the story is controlled by reactions to the threat of catastrophe, the catastrophe itself and the after-effects of the catastrophe.

Story spicers are necessary for plot fulfillment here. In *The Plague*, Camus uses rescue as a continuing device to dramatize the plight of those caught in the horror because it is the struggle to free themselves from the plague that constitutes the thrust of the story. In fact, in just about every story where catastrophe is a plot motivator, the spicer, rescue, will be present. And, in the same way, the plot motivator, survival, will usually be there too. Will he/she survive the catastrophe? Will he/she be rescued? These questions are necessary parts of the plot, but the focus is on the catastrophe itself, on the series of disasters and calamities, with rescue and survival playing an integral, though subordinate, role. It really comes down to a question of emphasis.

Now, suppose we take a natural catastrophe and enlarge it with a man-made catastrophe, a double dip so-to-speak. Here again the same general principles apply. Survival is part of the circumstances, but we continue with major emphasis on the catastrophe. In John Steinbeck's *Grapes of Wrath*, we have a natural catastrophe, the dust-bowl-drought in Oklahoma in the nineteen thirties, and the man-made catastrophe, the Great Depression, fusing to become a double-layered event that questions the very nature of capitalism and social justice. Are injustice and oppression and misery natural products beyond our control, or can man do something about his lot? Are we, each of us, individual islands of self-concern or are we inexorably tied to one another, interdependent and all part of a greater whole?

The *Grapes of Wrath* is the story of the Joad family's journey from their barren Oklahoma farm to the promise of migratory farm work in California. Without catastrophe as the plot motivator, the story would become little more than a travelogue, but because Steinbeck has given the plot substance by means of the series of disasters and calamities that befall the Joad family, the story is exciting, provoking, moving and forceful.

The Joad family caravan consists of three generations comprising eleven people plus an ex-preacher named Jim Casy. They travel west by means of a barely serviceable truck, and with vivid descriptive passages Steinbeck paints the misery of the drought-filled land, as well as the folly of the farmers who stayed and tried to stem the inevitable until their land was claimed by an avaricious bank-foreclosure system. On the first night west, Grampa Joad dies from a stroke and soon the truck breaks down and delays them. They meet others returning from California who say there is no more work to be had, that the conditions are worse than in Oklahoma. But the Joads travel on, spurred by their own dreams of a welcoming California.

By the time the family reaches the first migrant camp in California they have lost Noah, the mentally retarded son, who wanders off when the family is bathing in a river, and Gramma Joad who dies as the family goes across the desert at night. At the migrant camp the family finds there really is no work. And the family moves on, until eventually they come to a large farm where they do some picking. But agitators are there, trying to convince the pickers not to work because the wages are too low. The Joads are desperate, though, and they sign up and are escorted by police to the farm where they pick for an entire day and earn enough for just one meal. Tom Joad, the son, gets into a scrap with the police, and the family must try and hide him. So they flee again, and this time they hole up with other migrants in an abandoned boxcar along a stream. Tom's presence is disclosed, and Ma Joad sends him away for his own safety. Then the autumn rains begin, and the daughter, Rose of Sharon, gives birth to a dead baby. Soon the stream overflows and the boxcars are flooded. The family must flee again, only this time the rains have made their old vehicle useless. So they go off on foot and find an old barn in which they also find a boy and his starving father. Rose of Sharon, with milk in her breasts, feeds the starving man, and in this way, Steinbeck is saying the poor sustained one another during this terrible catastrophe.

In a book as encompassing as *The Grapes of Wrath*, there are bound to be at least several plot motivators. There are elements of persecution here (as mirrored in the attitudes of the authorities and the landowners who want nothing more than to exploit and humiliate the "okies"). There is survival, sometimes against overwhelming odds. To an extent, also, we can see the use of searching, in the sense that the Joads are seeking some permanent, tranquil resting place. But catastrophe is what moves this plot, and it reasserts itself on almost every page.

As for story spicers, we can find clear use of authority, in the sense that the Joads continually run afoul of it; the quest for material well-being — in this case as a source of food, shelter and money; honor and dishonor in that a man can find true worth by joining his fellow man to better their common lot. He honors himself and his fellow man in the process.

Many have traced the plot of the *Grapes of Wrath* to The Bible — specifically to the Book of Exodus. In both instances the story concerns people led into the wilderness with the hope of something better, in a search for a "promised land." Both stories open with the presence of catastrophic conditions. In The Bible, the Egyptian Pharaoh is refusing to allow Moses to lead the Israelites out of Egypt and as a result The Lord visits a series of calamities on the countryside. In one night all the Egyptian cattle die. A hailstorm kills off mature herbs and trees in the fields. A plague of locusts ruins any remaining vegetable and fruit plants. And then come three days of inky black darkness. Finally, after The Lord and Moses set up the Feast of the Passover and every Egyptian first-born dies, the Pharaoh lets the people go. For John Steinbeck this is the blueprint for the *Grapes of Wrath*. His plot has its own tortuous turns and twists, but the essential story is the same: catastrophe motivating a journey for some kind of redemption.

War has been a fertile source of catastrophe stories for as long as man has told tales. In the works of the ancient Greeks and up to fairly modern time, war was written about in individual terms, showing the exploits or the crimes of one person against another, minus a background of general suffering. For many centuries war was an adventurous pursuit, more to be gloried in than despised, and individual heroes and villains emerged through legend and the pages of literature. War wasn't catastrophic, or at least it wasn't presented that way. It was more an opportunity to judge the souls of men. What suffering and horror occurred was confined to individual circumstances, such as depicted in the tragedies of Shakespeare and in the Homeric epics.

It is in the nineteenth century that war is first treated realistically. Tolstoi does so in *War and Peace*, his monumental work about Napoleon's invasion of Russia. Stephen Crane in 1895 wrote *The Red Badge of Courage* which probes the psychological reactions of a young soldier to battle during the fiercest fighting of the Civil War. Crane lays out the horror of war in general, the death and destruction of young men by the thousands, the smell and the look of a battlefield, and what it is like to be there. The graphic telling of the catastrophe of war and what it does to those who fight in it dispelled the long-held notion that war could be a glorious exercise and a heady pursuit of adventure. "War is hell!" General William Sherman said, and Crane showed that to be true.

In the twentieth century the wars have produced literature that expands on realistic themes. The sense of catastrophe that flows from Erich Maria Remarque's *All Quiet on the Western Front* is generated by the wanton death and destruction in the trenches of the First World War. The year it appeared (1929), Ernest Hemingway's novel, *A Farewell to Arms* came out expressing the same sentiments. It is the story of an American ambulance driver in Italy during the war and his love affair with an English nurse. Hemingway describes the horrors of the fighting as the Allies retreat from Caporetto. He flashes to us the realism and the catastrophe that is war. The English nurse becomes pregnant, and the American deserts duty and travels with her to Switzerland where she dies in childbirth. In the end the catastrophe of war has claimed them both.

In our modern age, of course, it is nuclear catastrophe that we face, and ever since the atomic age became reality in 1945, writers have spewed forth literature based on its possibilities. What if?... What if?... Actually, it was in 1914 that it was mentioned first — by H.G. Wells, in *The World Set Free:*

> The catastrophe of the atomic bombs which shook men out of cities and businesses and economic relations, shook them also out of their old-established habits of thought, and out of the lightly held beliefs and prejudices that came down to them from the past.

Since 1945 it's been what if...

> ...we have already had World War III, the major cities of the United States are destroyed and a small town in Florida, cut off from the rest of the world, tries to cope by reversion to a primitive lifestyle? *Alas Babylon*, by Pat Frank, 1959.

> ...we have a set of bombers flying towards Moscow because of a defective missile-alarm system, and there is no way to recall them? *Fail-Safe*, by Eugene Burdick and Harvey Wheeler, 1962.

> ...an obsessed Red Chinese Colonel plots to drop a nuclear bomb on New York City and provoke total war? *Thirty Seconds Over New York*, by Robert Buchard, 1970.

> ...a scientist dies at Los Alamos in 1946 of radiation sickness and during the eight days of his dying his colleagues discuss and weigh the consequences of producing and using the bomb? *The Accident*, by Dexter Master, 1975.

Perhaps the classic use of catastrophe in our nuclear age is found in Nevil Shute's *On The Beach*, published in 1963. Here, as with almost all the literature in which catastrophe is a plot motivator, there is also the motivator survival. Yet is is the catastrophe itself that spurs the story on. A "short, bewildering war" in the Northern Hemisphere has resulted in the annihilation of all human life there, and now the heavy, lethal cloud of radiation is making its way inexorably towards Australia, with Melbourne the last major city as yet unaffected. There are about nine months left before radiation will blot out every living thing.

The major character is Dwight Towers, an American and commanding officer of the U.S.S. *Scorpion*, an atom-powered submarine, who stands firm against the impending doom, preserving his allegiance to his country and his family even though both are now gone. As the available options for continued life slowly cease to exist, Towers still searches for some straw of life, and in this we see the overpowering urge to survive that the author waves before us. The catastrophe of nuclear holocaust is so complete, however, that one by one each of the characters succumbs until finally there is no one and nothing left.

Then, of course, the real — and final — catastrophe dawns... the end of all known life.

5

Love and Hate

"Muse, tell me the deeds of golden Aphrodite," begins an ancient hymn, "who stirs up sweet passion in the gods and subdues the tribes of mortal men and birds that fly in the air and all the many creatures that the dry land rears and all that the sea..."

Ah, Aphrodite, the Greek Goddess of Love, the embodiment of man's passion and desire, the agent of man's joy and rapture. Legend has it that she's the daughter of Zeus and Dione, taking shape in the foam of the surging sea that erupts around the severed genital organ of Uranus, the God of Heaven. She lands, first, at Cythera and then at Cyprus and as she comes ashore, the land grows alive beneath her feet.

In Aphrodite the Greeks had a vehicle for the full expression of love, and the legends of her powers grew many and varied. Both Sophocles and Euripedes describe her omnipotence over gods and men and the powerlessness of those opposing her. The poet Lucretius adds his voice as well: "Yea, through seas and mountains and tearing rivers and the leafy haunts of birds and verdant plains thou dost strike fond love into the hearts of all, and makest them in hot desire to renew the stock of their races, each after his own kind."

The idea of love — and hate — is clearly represented in the ancient literature. After all, it is Aphrodite who really sets in motion the events leading to the Trojan War. Paris is asked to judge a contest of beauty among three of the goddesses: Athena, Hera and Aphrodite. He chooses Aphrodite, and in return she offers him the most beautiful mortal woman in the world. Paris wants Helen, the wife of Menelaus, King of Athens, and steals her away. Then he is challenged to a duel by Menelaus, a duel he would never win because he is not a fighter. In truth, he is a lover. Enter Aphrodite... she sweeps him up and places him in his bedchamber, eager, anticipatory, ready!

Aphrodite then disguises herself as an old servant and goes to Helen and whets her appetite for Paris. Soon, it's Helen who goes to Paris, and they make warm, passionate love.

While Aphrodite smiles at what she has created and relishes the beauty prize Paris has bestowed on her.

Helen accompanies Paris to Troy, Menelaus fumes over his wife's treachery and soon the armies of Athens and other Greek city-states begin their march on Troy. And the ten years of the Trojan War begin.

Now, let's update this drama about three thousand years. What if... the ultimate male fantasy is to make love with the most beautiful, desirable woman in the world; and what if... four men come together and agree that the object of their longing is a gorgeous, sexy movie queen named Sharon Fields, the embodiment of all their unfulfilled desires; and what if... they hatch a plan to kidnap this movie queen in order to play out their untamed sexual fantasies; and what if... after the kidnapping they install Sharon Fields in a mountain cabin and then fall to bickering among themselves; and what if... Sharon Fields becomes the object of a wide search and she and her kidnappers are beseiged in their mountain cabin; and what if... one of the kidnappers falls madly in love with her...

What we have here is the plot of *The Fan Club*, a 1974 novel by Irving Wallace. Did Wallace purloin the essentials of the famous story about Helen of Troy? Perhaps, but so what? Actually what Wallace has done is to take the Helen of Troy story further and in a different direction. In *The Fan Club* we concentrate on the interrelationships between Sharon Fields and her kidnappers. In *The Iliad*, where we find the details of Helen's kidnapping, emphasis is on the fortunes of the contending armies and their champions. Homer did not dwell too much on just how Helen and Paris actually do get along — on their daily conversations and such. But not so in *The Fan Club*. We come to know each of the kidnappers intimately, and we see clearly their motivations and desires. In the process we also come to know Sharon Fields intimately, more intimately perhaps than anyone could ever know Homer's Helen of Troy.

Yet the essentials of the two stories remain the same: a beautiful, desirable woman is kidnapped, the consequences start a chain of events that have destructive results for all concerned. For Paris, Helen and Menelaus there are the ten years of the Trojan War; for Sharon Fields and her kidnappers, there is only degradation, distaste and ultimately, for the kidnappers, death.

Even though love reigns in the Greek legends, there is hate, too. The Greeks and their gods hated as fiercely as they loved. "No Olympian god is so hated... he thinks only of strife and wars and battles..." Homer writes of the god, Ares in *The Iliad*. Ares is the spirit of carnage, the slayer of men, interested only in blood and death and slaughter. He may be one of the divine gods, but in Greek legend none has less respect from the other gods and none is so feared and despised. Throughout *The Iliad* his partiality for the Trojans is apparent, and Homer describes him in less than glowing terms.

But the clearest object of his hate was another god, or in this case, a goddess, Athena. "I begin to sing of Pallas Athena," goes one of the ancient *Homeric Hymns*, "the glorious goddess, owl-eyed, inventive, unbending of heart, pure virgin, savior of cities, courageous... From his awful head wise Zeus himself bore her arrayed in warlike arms of flashing gold, and awe seized all the gods as they gazed..."

Athena is the spirit of the warrior, yet she is not war hungry, as is Ares. She might urge the Greeks on in battle if their morale were to drop, she might inspire them to heroic deeds. She is at all times rational and protective — unlike Ares who is destructive and demonic. Homer writes of Athena with great passion and respect, and Odysseus, his most famous character, is the object of Athena's constant love and protection.

But there is hate between Ares and Athena, based as much on their conflicting natures as anything else. The bloodthirsty Ares versus the noble Athena. They have a battle in the twenty-first book of *The Iliad*, and it will be the only real contest they fight. But the hatred between them is palpable. Diomedes, the Greek hero of numerous battles, finds himself face to face with Ares, and the blood-lust of the god is a vicious thing to behold. Athena, who has come to the aid of Diomedes in other situations, sees his peril and appears to him in the flesh, leaping on his chariot and taking the place of his driver. Ares throws his spear at Diomedes, but Athena deflects it almost casually. And then, injecting her power into the spear-throw of Diomedes, she causes Ares to be deeply wounded and to go howling off in pain.

If the gods can hate one another, man can also. Hate is hardly relegated to the divine circle. And as a plot motivator it can have a powerful force on a story line, just as love can. Hate and love, as opposites, can usually deal with the same set of circumstances and motivate the plot in separate directions. For example, let's go back to *The Fan Club*. What if... Sharon Fields is kidnapped, not because she is a love goddess, but because she is a hated symbol! Perhaps in the way the Symbionese Liberation Army treated Patty Hearst in 1974. Now, after the kidnapping, the hatred begins to pour out. Anger, even physical abuse, may occur. (In *The Fan Club* it took the form of sexual abuse.) We come to know the kidnappers intimately, and the person kidnapped. The kidnappers bicker among themselves, violence erupts, and finally there is death and destruction. All arising out of hatred, not love. Same set of circumstances, same number of characters, same outcome. Same plot motivator, too — but in mirror image!

As a plot motivator love is most effective when it is in motion — that is, when it expands or contracts or takes on a different aspect. Love should never be static, it must have a life of its own! Then the story will move, as well. The same is true of hate.

Look at how Ernest Hemingway deals with love in *A Farewell to Arms*, his 1929 novel set in Italy during the First World War. Though the book has anti-war overtones, it is first and foremost a love story. Lieutenant Frederick Henry, a young American with an Italian ambulance unit, meets Catherine Barkley, a British hospital nurse. At first there is just casual interest in one another, but then Henry becomes wounded and is moved to a hospital in Milan. Catherine is there, too, and they fall in love. Catherine manages to be with him constantly, and he slowly recuperates. They dine in cozy little restaurants, ride the countryside in a carriage and become closer and closer. From time to time Catherine comes to his hospital room where they make love.

Then, Henry is due to go back to the front, his wound now healed. They spend his last days and nights together in a hotel where Catherine tells him she is now pregnant. Henry is deeply upset about leaving her in the midst of war, but she assures him she will be all right. He goes back to his unit and soon finds himself in the middle of some of the heaviest fighting. The Italian army begins the ill-fated retreat from Caporetto which ends in a chaotic frenzy of disorder, and Henry must try to cope and save himself. As the retreat continues Henry comes to the conclusion that he has no place in the war, and he sets out on his own back to Milan and Catherine. When he gets there, he discovers that the British nurses have gone to Stresa, and he then borrows some civilian clothes from a friend and makes it to Stresa where he finally locates Catherine. The bartender at the hotel where he and Catherine are staying warns him the authorities will arrest him the next day for desertion. He offers Henry and Catherine his dingy for an escape to Switzerland. All night Henry rows, and by morning his hands are so raw that Catherine insists on taking over. Henry protests, but to no avail, and they finally reach Switzerland. They spend the next few months at an inn outside Montreux, and they discuss marriage. But Catherine will not be married while she is pregnant. They make plans to be together after the war ends.

Then it is time for Catherine to have the baby, and after hours of labor, the baby is born dead. Catherine begins to hemorrhage, and as Henry sits with her, she dies. For Henry it is the end. There is no place he can go, no one to talk to, nothing he can do. As he leaves the hospital and walks back to his hotel it is raining.

A tragic love story about a love that grows, blossoms and finally ends. It doesn't die, it just ends. The love has a life of its own in this story, and that is the key to using love as a plot motivator. Hemingway referred to *A Farewell to Arms* as his *Romeo and Juliet*, and there are certainly similarities. While Shakespeare plays his story out against a backdrop of family feuding and some political turmoil, Hemingway sets his story in wartime. When we think of classic love stories, of course, *Romeo and Juliet* comes immediately to mind, and if there are star-crossed lovers in Shakespeare's drama, is it any less so for Hemingway, just because *A Farewell to Arms* is set in the twentieth century? Henry and Catherine are equally beset by a hostile environment, they carve out their love in the midst of all that turmoil, they pledge themselves to one another, and their love never dies. It simply ends.

The story spicers Hemingway uses are just two — honor and dishonor, and searching. It's well recognized that in every Hemingway work we'll get a taste of honor and dishonor. From his impotent veteran, Jake Barnes in *The Sun Also Rises* to Santiago, his grizzled fisherman in *The Old Man and the Sea*, Hemingway rolls with concepts of honor and dishonor. Courage and grace and bravery under fire are all part of the mosaic, and *A Farewell to Arms* is no exception. How does Henry deal with combat? How does Henry deal with being wounded? How does Henry deal with a woman who tells him she is pregnant? How does Henry deal with survival in the midst of chaos and frenzy? Does he honor himself? Does he perform with grace?

And then there's the element of searching in this book. The search for love, the search for sanctuary, the search for peace and an absence of war, the search for rationality in the midst of the madness of war and killing. Imagine the story without this added element. The characters would become one dimensional as they simply "experience" the events without trying to apply any type of value judgment. Hemingway has given added life to his story by giving the element of searching aspect to the plot; the characters are on the move; they *want* something; they *need* something; they are looking to *find* something. They search.

As strong as love is on one side of the question, hate can be equally as strong on the other. Would someone really write a book about hate? Isn't it so... distasteful, uncomfortable and such a sincerely loathesome subject?

Perhaps, but that's not to say it can't also make a good story. Hate as a plot motivator has a built-in advantage: the very nature of hate is conflict and tension. When we hate, we are at swords' points. And any good writer will say that stories need conflict and tension; without them a piece of work is hardly more than a piece of fluff.

So, a good story can come in any size or shape, wrapped in all manner of ribbons. Watch...

A young man thinking he is in love marries a woman somewhat higher on the social ladder. Up to this point in his life he has always thought of himself as graceless, a peasant-like individual whom no one could ever like, and he is overwhelmed by his love for his new wife. Only... after they are married she tells him she has been in love with someone else before she met him, and he is crushed. She only married him so she could live well, he thinks. It's the only reason anyone would ever want to marry him! Slowly, as the years pass he develops a persecution mania. And he becomes richer and richer. He ignores his wife, has a series of cheap love affairs, and has nothing but contempt for his children and subsequent grandchildren. Finally, after he has been married for 45 years, he decides to disinherit his entire family and give his money to his illigitimate son. He has grown hard and mean, and he has no friends, no sentimental attachments. He hates his family, and they in turn hate him. He turns to his illigitimate son but finds that here, too, he is disappointed. The man is weak and will no doubt be under the thumb of other family members. And so he dies, unlamented, heartily disliked, and understood by almost no one. For the rest of the family it is simply the end of a long curse.

Clearly, this story, *Viper's Tangle*, by Francois Mauriac, is the product of a collision between love and hate. Hate wins, of course, and the plot is motivated by its continual application. A bombardment of hate page after page may be a bitter pill for some, yet it makes a good story because the hate is never static. It moves! It grows! It changes direction! In spite of the distasteful feelings aroused. Somehow we are interested.

But a story filled with hate can just as easily be filled with love — even obsessive love. A 1979 novel by Scott Spencer, *Endless Love*, shows us how.

A seventeen-year-old boy, David, and a sixteen-year-old girl, Jade, are madly, madly in love. Their love affair grows so intense that David is forbidden to see Jade for 30 days, and in retaliation he sets fire to Jade's parents' home. David, the son of left-wing former members of the Communist party, is caught and sentenced to a mental institution for a period of three years. Jade, whose parents are trendy and not very political, is distraught, and suffers as the family slowly breaks apart. Years go by and David, now out on parole, still hungers after Jade, obsessively, compulsively. He violates his parole and locates her in New York, and when they are reunited, they resume their lovemaking, to which the author devotes 35 pages. Before David locates Jade, however, he has accidentally caused the death of her father, and the police are now after him. In the end David is lost, cut off from his family, from society, even from Jade, all because of the obsessive nature of his love.

Just as with *Viper's Tangle*, we have a superabundance of plot motivator in *Endless Love*. In one case it was hate, now it is love. The first time David and Jade make love, for instance, they do so on an old double mattress scented with Chanel No. 5. Most of David's waking moments are spent thinking about Jade, fantasizing about her or making love with her. For David it is an obsession bordering on madness, but clearly it is the one thing that gives meaning to his life.

And doesn't *that* sound familiar? In Francois Mauriac's work, the only thing that gives meaning to his leading character's life is his deep hatred for the members of his family. It's what motivates the plot, and as he grows more bitter with time, his feelings consume him to the point of obsession.;

Love and hate — two sides of the same coin.

6

The Chase

"There he goes!" The shout rings out, and action speeds up. The chase is on, and if it's done well enough, we'll identify with those doing the chasing or those being chased. It's a simple formula for a good story. There's conflict (why else would there be a chase?), there's movement and there's a natural story line. The chase itself could be the entire story in that it would comprise a beginning, a middle and an end, and we could weave a complete plot through it. That's essentially what Jules Verne does with *Around the World In Eighty Days*, his saga of Phineas Fogg who races his arch rival in a variety of contraptions for a prize put up by a New York newspaper. The chase is for the title of winner, and is to be completed within the prescribed time. The entire story deals with the race — the chase — but in the course of it Verne weaves in love and adventure and scientific know-how. Without the chase there simply would not have been a story.

The chase as a plot motivator seems to work best where stories lend themselves to adventure, mystery, suspense. The reasons are obvious: the necessary ingredients of a chase include action and conflict, and the writer has a fertile opportunity to stretch out the chase or narrow it by creating tight escapes or despair or even temporary capture. Each time, the tension between the characters is heightened because the chase gets down to a basic human level, an eyeball-to-eyeball confrontation. Each close brush gives us more to identify with in the characters, and it provides additional fuel to stoke up the fires of suspense, mystery or adventure.

When is a chase *not* a chase?

When the object of the chase is already there, in place, waiting to be captured. This is more like a search, a quest, because no one is running away, no one is trying to elude capture. Using the chase as a plot motivator means that someone (or something) is *after* someone else, and the latter is or should be aware of it. That awareness, in fact, creates the tensions that add up to suspense: will he/she be caught? How does he/she get away?

Among chase stories the absolute classic is Victor Hugo's *Les Misérables*, written in 1862. Basically, it is the story of Jean Valjean who is sentenced to five years in prison because he steals a loaf of bread to feed his starving sister and her family. After several attempts to escape are thwarted, his sentence is extended until he is finally released, nineteen years later. He spends a night with the Bishop of Digne and repays the hospitality by stealing the Bishop's sliverware. The police catch him, return him to the Bishop who refuses to prosecute, and in fact adds the silver candlesticks to the booty. "Use this silver as a means to lead an honest life," the Bishop urges him.

Several years later, Valjean, now posing as Father Madeleine, runs a glass factory in a small provincial town. Father Madeleine's background is known to no one. He is a mystery man and has excited the attention of Monsieur Javert, the police inspector, who has an obsession to find out about him. Father Madeleine is a kind and generous man and employs many citizens of the town. He is also reputed to have prodigious strength. One day Javert, who keeps close watch over him, sees Father Madeleine lift a cart to save the life of an old man who has fallen under it. Javert remembers that in prison, where he grew up, there was one person who had just such strength — the bread thief, Jean Valjean.

Javert reports this fact to the Paris police who advise that they already have a Jean Valjean in custody and that he will be tried in two days. Javert confesses his error to Father Madeleine who immediately realizes the wrong man is in jail. He goes to the Paris police and identifies himself as Jean Valjean. Javert comes and arrests him, and he goes to prison — only to escape one day later.

Now the chase is on. Javert's obsession with Valjean causes him to track his quarry from town to town, day after day, year after year. Each time Javert gets close, Valjean escapes, and for a while he lives in the Gorbeau tenement on the outskirts of Paris, another time he lives as the helper to a convent gardener, and finally he returns to live quietly on a side street in Paris. Here he makes new friends, though one of them will eventually turn him in to Javert. But once again, when Javert appears, Valjean is able to escape, while leaving his false friend behind to be arrested.

Some time later a political revolt by the left breaks out in Paris, and there is a rush to the barricades. Valjean, in the course of searching for a friend, discovers Javert bound and held as a spy by the revolutionists. There is no question he will be executed. Valjean, however, frees him, and then hides in the Paris sewers. He is urged to come to the surface by the same false friend who had turned him in to Javert before. And as he pokes his head into the streets, there, once again, is Javert. Valjean is arrested on the spot, but when Valjean requests to carry a wounded friend's body inside his house before going off to prison, Javert has an overwhelming attack of conscience. Unwilling to imprison the man who had saved his life, Javert bolts for the Seine where he jumps in and drowns himself. The chase, now, is over.

There has been some indication that what Hugo is presenting, with the story of Jean Valjean, is not only a social commentary about slum life in the first third of the nineteenth century in France — a true picture of misery, despair and poverty — but also a loose parellel with the life of Jesus Christ, as set forth in the Bible. Valjean is certainly not a religious figure, but in his misery, in the betrayal of his innocence, not once but over and over again, and in his obsessive determination to make things right by Javert we have the classic conflict of the good man done in by self-righteous authority. Wasn't Jesus Christ on the receiving end of false accusation after false accusation? Wasn't he befriended and betrayed? Wasn't his life's purpose to help his fellow man? Wasn't he able to perform physical feats no other man could do? Was he not subjected to inhumane treatment by the authorities?

All of these things befall Jean Valjean. We ask ourselves... did Victor Hugo steal the plot of the life of Jesus Christ? There are differences, of course: Christ was frail and saintly, Valjean husky with superhuman strength; Christ was propounding a religion, Valjean merely wants to live quietly and freely; Christ acquired disciples, Valjean is a lone man fighting a lonely battle. But the authorities chase Christ just as they chase Valjean, and in the end the other worldly attributes of both men far outdistance the petty concerns of their accusers. The goodness in mankind triumphs.

The chase action in *Les Misérables* motivates a plot based on the arduous trials of a good man in the face of unfairness, deception, treachery and obsession. Without the chase we would have little more than an academic treatise on the misery of slum life in Paris in the early nineteenth century. The chase makes what is essentially a social commentary into an exciting, vibrant story. It establishes two things for us: the basic conflict that every good plot needs, and an opportunity to identify with either or both of the characters. In the course of the book we come to know Javert almost as well as we know Valjean, and we understand his obsession to see Valjean behind bars in the same reasonable terms that we understand Valjean's obsession to avoid imprisonment.

This is good story writing, and it makes us appreciate the fact that characters and their times are not so black and white as we might have thought. No character is all good or all bad. There are redeeming qualities in everyone. In *Les Misérables* the chase shows that this is true.

Not all chase stories involve the one doing the chasing — the chas*er* — hunting down the chas*ee*. Occasionally the chasee does most of the chasing within his own head. He chases himself until he is caught.

In this, a "psychological" novel in that much of the chase, or hunt, takes place in the character's mind, what he thinks and why he thinks it are more important than the physical action of escape or capture.

This is the core of perhaps the most substantial psychological novel of all time, Fyodor Dostoevski's *Crime and Punishment* which first appeared in 1866. It is the story of a brilliant student, Raskolnikov, who commits a crime — a double murder — because he reasons that he has a moral right to do away with those who are his inferiors, in this case a widowed pawnbroker and her stepsister. I'll put them out of their misery, he tells himself. It's for their own good, and the jewels I steal from them will help my education. We'll all be better off for this!

Then he receives a summons from the police. I'm caught, he thinks, they know all about it... where did I go wrong?

But the police don't ask him about the murders. He owes a debt to his landlady, and the police want him to pay it. So relieved at this unexpected reprieve, Raskolnokov collapses and must be revived. The police ask a few more questions, but he is in a confused state, and his answers are strange enough to provoke mild suspicion. The police let him go, however.

He returns to his room where he falls into bed with a high fever and remains for four days. When he recovers, he finds out the police have been by to see him and that they talked to him. He can't remember what he said, but he knows the suspicions have grown.

He forces himself to go outside for some air, and his agitation is reduced when he sees a newspaper with its account of the double murder he has committed. As he reads the story, a stranger — a detective — joins him, and once more Raskolnikov becomes agitated. He talks too much about the crime, inadvertently revealing that he might in fact be the murderer. But, except for his suspicious statements, there is no hard evidence linking him with the crime, and he walks away unimpeded.

Then he is called to the police station, and he faces Porfiry, the chief of the murder investigation. Questioned about the crime, he denies his guilt, yet the phrasing of the questions and the sardonic responses to his answers torture his conscience. They must *know*, his anguished mind screams. They're just toying with me before they arrest me...

Partly to justify himself he begins to explain his general theory that for a man of genius, such as himself, any means whatsoever are appropriate to allow a continuation of life and study. He implies that even murder is justified if it permits a man of genius added knowledge and experience.

Once again he is released for lack of hard evidence. But the heavy burden of police suspicion and his own growing paranoia keep his mind in a state of turmoil. They *know*!... they *must* know...

And so he returns to the police station intending to find out for sure. But once again Porfiry toys with him, asking questions with such sardonic certainty that Raskolnikov is ready to come apart at the seams. At no time does Porfiry make a direct accusation. He implies, he suggests, but he doesn't point a finger. Raskolnikov, though, is now thoroughly frightened, and his emotional stability is severely cracked. He is suffering greatly, but he is allowed to leave the police station.

Shortly thereafter, his mind by now tortured almost beyond endurance with guilt and shame, he confesses what he has done to a friend, and he is overheard by her next-door neighbor. The neighbor confronts him with the knowledge, but still he can't bring himself to confess to Porfiry, who by now tells him he knows he is the murderer.

Then his family reassure him that no matter what he has done, they will stand by him and love him forever. Only now does he confess, and the chase inside his own head finally is over.

Although the police are clearly involved in this story right from the beginning, the hunt actually takes place inside Raskolnikov's mind. Porfiry is like a stage manager, using questions and answers and atmosphere to create an environment that would encourage the confession. But Raskolnikov's conscience is the hunter and his superego the quarry. The chase takes place within the confines of a moral equation: is there a limit on free will and need one suffer in order to understand it? Dostoevski answers yes to both questions.

If we set up a hunting story, the chase is the most important plot motivator. Story spicers such as searching and rescue come naturally into play because a hunt implies a search and rescue. But there is this difference: with a search the quarry is often someone or something that hasn't done anything wrong. They may or may not want to be found, but it isn't because they are trying to elude capture. With a chase, of course, the opposite is true. The quarry is trying to avoid capture, is trying to get away and not be found. Searching stories also involve someone looking to be found, someone who has been lost or abandoned. Not so with chase stories.

Thus, if we use a hunting motif for a chase story, we ought to be able to understand the confines of the motivator. And, of course, one of the most famous hunting stories has to be Herman Melville's *Moby Dick*, the obsessive hunt for the white whale. More chase stories than we imagine pattern themselves on *Moby Dick* — and for good reason. The conflict is between man and animal, good and evil; the characters are outsized, dangerous; and the motivation is pure obsession, a lust for vengeance rarely equalled throughout literature. These are the ingredients for a rich and lively tale.

Take Walter Clark's 1950 novel, *The Track of the Cat*, a thinly disguised reincarnation of *Moby Dick*. The Bridges family live in a remote Nevada valley on a large cattle ranch at the turn of the century. Word comes that a huge black panther (translate: white whale) has been killing their cattle in the mountains, and the two oldest Bridges brothers set off to kill it as the first snowstorm of the year settles in. First one and then the second brother is killed by the panther, and so the third and last brother and a mystical, legend-spouting Indian take up the chase. Before it's over, the hunters become the hunted as the cold and the panther's cunning and the lack of food take their toll. The blackness of the panther is evil incarnate, of course, but the irony in this story is more direct: the third brother is frail and abhors killing while his older brothers relish it. Yet in the end it is the third brother who finally kills the panther. (Unlike Captain Ahab who is finally done in by his white whale. But then, isn't Walter Clark just applying a what if... scenario?)

Chase stories don't always have to be so serious or ponderous. They can be cast in the adventure, suspense or mystery mode and still make us laugh. Story spicers such as suspicion, even suicide or criminal action can be added, and the action can be light with humor spilling from the pages. This is what Thomas Berger does with *Who Is Teddy Villanova?* — a 1977 novel that is really a spoof of the detective mystery. The protagonist is Russel Wren, a former English literature professor turned private eye who tries throughout the entire book to prove that he is *not* Teddy Villanova, an arch fiend and international criminal. The story of the chase is just this: Wren's hunt for Teddy Villanova or for information that will prove, first, that he is not Teddy Villanova and second, just who and where Teddy Villanova really is. In the course of the book, Wren consistently avoids his secretary's demands for back pay, is knocked around over and over, is questioned repeatedly by the police, is held at gun point and is generally one of the most ineffective private eyes to cross the detective, mystery, suspense scene.

The spoof continues in the way Wren speaks: with outlandish, flowery, Victorian phrasing, overblown and often quite pointless. He is the antithesis of the hard-boiled, no-nonsense operative who speaks little but acts with great verve and success. He is the chronic loser, and even when he is hired to find Teddy Villanova, the amount he is offered is insultingly small. Near the end of the book, Berger has Wren saying, ''I still don't understand the part I've played, but I assure you, I'm nursing a massive grudge against someone.'' In this we see the essence of his ineffectuality. He doesn't even know who his enemy is! Yet the chase goes on and the chuckles pile up.

Though the heart of most chase stories involve the hunt, sometimes the chase isn't to capture the quarry so much as to expose and thereby render the quarry ineffective. The purpose of a chase is to generate action, to move the story along, and the end doesn't have to be so perfect. The chase itself is what motivates the plot, not the ultimate result.

This is the way things happened in *The Bedford Incident*, a cold-war drama written by Mark Rascovich and published in

1963. The author pondered — what if... *The Bedford*, an American destroyer on duty in the North Atlantic, comes in contact with a Russian submarine trying to penetrate U.S. radar defense, and what if... the captain of *The Bedford* knows he can't fire on the submarine but must try and make the spying mission as difficult as possible, and what if... *The Bedford* is the most modern electronically equipped killing machine in the Navy and the submarine an equally equipped marvel in the Russian submarine services...

The Bedford's captain, Erik Finlander, is a veteran of the Second World War and an insatiable foe of submarines ever since the destroyer he sailed on in the war had been sunk. Once contact with the Russian submarine has been established, Finlander drives his ship and his crew to frightening lengths in order to win the only battle open to them — ship-handling dexterity. He hopes to force the sub to surface and thereby admit the superiority of Finlander's vessel and skill.

But as the conflict increases in intensity, the tension aboard *The Bedford* grows as well. Tacitly, both ship and submarine wage a bitter maneuvering battle with more and more control of the struggle given over to electronic devices that make them both lethal killing machines. In the end both ship and submarine perish, the victims of humans having too much power at their command without a corresponding check on the human frailties that can cause misjudgment in the use of that power.

Look carefully now... isn't that the ghost of *Moby Dick* peering through the pages of *The Bedford Incident*? The obsession of the captain for the undersea creature that almost destroyed him in his youth, the rising tension on board as the chase and the search continue for a quarry unseen but felt, the naked clash of good with evil (if, in fact, one considers the Russians the embodiment of evil. And at the height of the cold war, when *The Bedford Incident* was written, there was more general support for that view than there is today.)

The chase is on. . . "There he goes!" And with the spectre of *Moby Dick* hovering just barely in view, the story line is spiced by elements of search and rescue and deception and suspicion and honor and dishonor.

The hunt goes on, and the *Moby Dick* saga is stolen again.

7

Grief and Loss

Except in matters of love, there is probably no more universal theme in literature than death and its effect on those who have some thread of contact with the event. How do we react to death? How *should* we react? What to do next? What do we remember? Are our lives richer for knowing the deceased?

Questions like these are the fodder that causes dynamic stories to sprout. When we mourn, we aren't just feeling sad because someone we felt close to has died; we are marking the end of life for a part of us, as well. It is the part we shared with the deceased, that private part which contained special experiences and intimacies, special fantasies and unspoken dreams. No more will we hope or plan or wonder. We have only the reality of living to endure.

Death and the way it affects us is a powerful plot motivator because we can't run from it. We *must* stand and deal with it, we have no choice. From Aeschylus's *The Death of Achilles* right to Erich Segal's *Love Story* and beyond, the annals of literature are bulging with stories about death, or impending death, and our reactions to it. It is a superb technique for mirroring human values and human foibles because of the universality of the theme. The prospect of death — or the inevitability of it — or the fact of it — remains a constant throughout the story, and each character can be fleshed out and judged against the never varying constant. It is as if the story is bundled within a rolled-up carpet, and as we unroll the carpet the story unravels too, but never does it stray off the carpet. Grief and loss, which are the natural effects of death, preserve the constancy of it and cause the same reactions. If there is death, do we grieve? If we suffer a loss, do we hurt?

One way writers have dealt with this theme is to provide a kaleidoscope of characters and to weave their reactions and interreactions together against the backdrop of a central character's death or dying. Reactions differ, of course, just as individuals differ. Some are noble, some are coarse, some malicious, some just plain evil. None remain untouched, however, and in the interplay of their grief, we build a story.

Two great novelists fashioned stories this way, approximately a generation apart. Though they used the same mechanism, here we have one example when a plot is *not* stolen. As we'll see, there's just too much dissimilarity.

The first of these stories is William Faulkner's 1930 work, *As I Lay Dying*. It is the story of the dying and death of Addie Bundren and the way her husband, Anse Bundren, and her sons, Cash, Darl, Jewel and Vardaman, and her daughter, Dewey Dell, deal with it. As Addie lies propped in her bed, she can see out the window, and she watches her son, Cash, build the wooden coffin that will hold her. As he finishes a section he displays it for her approval, his only reason being an obsession with fine workmanship. Cash would be heartbroken if the coffin were irregularly finished. Addie has indicated she wishes to be buried in Jefferson, a town a full day's ride from the farm, and Anse is determined that her wish be fulfilled. But two other sons, Darl and Jewel, want to take a wagonload of lumber into town and earn three dollars for the family to use on the trip to Jefferson. At first Anse doesn't want them to make the trip, fearing they might not return in time to take Addie's body to Jefferson. But he finally gives in.

Then Addie dies, while the boys are still away and before Cash can finish the coffin. Vardaman, the youngest, returns to the house with a fish he has just caught, in time to be present during his mother's death throes. He entangles his mother's death with the death of the fish and he is severely upset.

Meanwhile, a torrential rainstorm has delayed Darl and Jewel with the lumber, and on top of that they must repair a broken wheel on the wagon. Cash, though, keeps working through the rain and finally finishes the coffin. As Addie's body is laid within it, Vardaman, who once almost suffocated in his crib, bores holes in the top of the coffin so his mother can get out.

There is a short graveside service and then the family begins the trek to Jefferson with Addie's body. Their destination is the family cemetery. But before they go very far, they come to the river, now swollen by the heavy rains. With a great deal of effort they succeed in getting the wagon with Addie's body almost across the river, when a huge log floats downstream and upsets the wagon. Cash's leg is broken in the melee, and he nearly drowns; the mules pulling the wagon are drowned, the coffin slips overboard but is finally collared and pulled to the bank.

Anse looks at the scattered remnants of his entourage, and he is tempted to ask a nearby farmer for the loan of a set of mules. But then he reconsiders...whatever is to carry Addie to her grave must be his and his alone. He will ask for no help from anyone. Instead, he offers to trade a spotted horse — a special favorite of Jewel's which he had worked morning and night to pay for — without asking Jewel if he could bargain it away. In this way Anse is able to get mules to continue the journey.

Jewel, however, is quite upset at what his father has done, and he hops on the spotted horse and rides off, leaving Anse's bargain for the mules hanging. But later Jewel has a change of heart, and without telling anyone in the family, he simply places the spotted horse in the barn of the person who has been bargaining with Anse for the mules.

By now Addie has been dead so long the buzzards are following the wagon. But still the family plunges on. It is nine days before they finally get Addie buried, and in the end it is Anse who is most rejuvenated by Addie's death. Before starting the trip home to the farm, he buys himself a new set of false teeth — something he has needed for a long time — and he has acquired a new wife. For each of the others, the death trip costs something precious: for Jewel it is his favorite horse; for Cash it is the use of his leg; for Darl it is his sanity (he sets fire to a barn where Addie's coffin lies the night before she is buried, and Anse turns him over to the authorities who send him to a nearby asylum). For Dewey Dell it is her self-respect, for a drugstore clerk seduces her by convincing her he has some medicine which can abort an illegitimate child she is carrying.

In the end, Faulkner has us believe that the roads through life and through death are not two separate paths but only one, and that it's absurd to try and distinguish between them. As Addie says on her deathbed: "I could just remember how my father used to say that the reason for living was to get ready to stay dead a long time."

Some quarter-century later James Agee deals with the same theme in his *A Death in the Family*. Again, we see the reactions of a host of characters to a single death. In this case it is the death of Jay Follett, husband, father, son, brother and respected citizen of Knoxville, Tennessee. It starts early one morning when Jay arises before daybreak to go to the bedside of his father who has been taken gravely ill. Jay and his wife, Mary, have a quiet breakfast together and decide not to wake their children, Rufus, who is six, and his younger sister, because Jay expects to be back by nightfall. But he doesn't come back, and Mary hears a stranger's voice say that Jay has been killed in an automobile accident. Agee then delves into how this death affects the various members of the family.

For Mary it is a cold slap of reality. Death is common, she comes to understand; many people suffer as she does. And she turns to her faith for consolation.

For Rufus, it is another of life's confusing moments such as his nightmares, or the reasons why older boys ask his name and then laugh and run away or why his mother has made him promise never to mention the color of a black maid's skin.

For Ralph Follet, Jay's brother and a drunk, who happens to be an undertaker, it provides a means for some small measure of self-worth. He will prepare his brother's body for burial; no one else will be allowed to do it.

With these and other characters Agee portrays efforts to understand Jay Follett's death in the grief and the love they share. The plot is simple — a man has died and we witness how those close to him react. The action, really, is in the portrayal of the reactions and how the feelings of the characters interweave, such as Rufus's urge to show off his new cap, bought for him by a great-aunt who wishes to ease the loss he will be feeling. He runs to his parents' bedroom but finds only his mother with face drawn and two pillows behind her back, his father's place empty. It's something a six-year-old boy just doesn't understand.

Story spicers in works like *As I Lay Dying* and *A Death in the Family* don't amount to much. We might fit in making amends, or honor and dishonor, but essentially, stories like these rely more on an exploration of emotion than on a connected series of events. Still, what plot there is will be spurred by the sense of grief and loss felt by each of the characters.

Let's be irreverent and call these "House of Death" books because that's what they really are. It's a fairly common story framework where the person who is dying or already dead and those the event affects are locked in close proximity with one another. The author weaves a story out of memory, fantasy and self-proof with the plot moving forward at a gradual pace.

This is what James T. Farrell does with *The Death of Nora Ryan*, a 1978 book about a woman who suffers a stroke and about her various children who gather by her lower-middle-class Chicago bedside and hold a vigil until she succumbs. Just as Faulkner and Agee do, Farrell has his characters develop in the light of the enveloping tragedy. There's Eddie the successful novelist, and Steve the successful doctor and Clara the sister who stayed at home... and an assortment of other siblings who spare time for their mother's death but who are barely touched by it all. In the end they return to their ordinary lives, their memories refreshed by thoughts of the way things used to be but their outlooks neither changed nor helped. They are the same people before the event as they are after it, and that, in itself, is the story. They are not ennobled by their mother's dying nor are they made more contemptible. Except in the immediate sense, the House of Death has little effect on them.

Now, what if... we have a dying character, and we want to focus, not on a whole range of people but on one only. Then, of course, there's more action to the plot because *something* has to happen to keep the plot moving. With a wide variety of characters, of course, the author can switch from person to person, introducing new ideas and new events as each new character is introduced. But with a single character this is most difficult. So the story line must move forward, from event to event, inexorably reaching the end. Take Hilma Wolitzer's 1974 book, *Ending*, the story of Sandy and Jay Kaufman, a couple in their early thirties who discover that Jay has terminal bone cancer. They have two children under five, and the story is of Sandy, mainly, and how she copes with the impending death. Her major decision is this: shall I dwell on the future and what it's going to be without him? Shall I gear myself to this? Or shall I ignore the future and let it take care of itself, and live in the present only?

She decides upon the latter, and the book shows what it's like to wait for Jay to die. Along the way, Wolitzer pinpoints certain things that sharpen the raw edges of grief, such as the cruelty of the nursing staff, the fact that there is now less laundry to do, the relish with which some people find interest in terminal death.

What does Sandy do to maintain some modest sense of equilibrium? Well, she tries out an encounter group, thinking it might cleanse and revitalize her; she gets it on with Mr. Caspar, an elderly neighbor who occasionally babysits — new steps in new directions, not so much to open up her life as to give her current existence a safety valve.

Sandy shows strength and compassion all at once: her doctor can't tell Jay he is dying, so Sandy takes up the responsibility. ''I wanted to do it while he was still able to walk. It seemed immoral somehow to tell a dying man the miserable and imminent truth when he was helpless. Lying down in the very path of the words.''

But this is Jay's story, too, and Wolitzer paints him with courage. In his last days, suffering and deeply in pain, he discovers that a young patient recovering from an appendectomy is a student of photography. Jay, a television cameraman, has a fulfilling avocation as an amateur still photographer, and so, in a final act of will, Jay discusses photography with the young patient and they exchange information and secret lore in the manner of those who truly understand and love their work. It is a final statement by Jay that he *is* someone, even in the face of death.

For Sandy the loss of Jay is something she refuses to focus on until he is gone; for Jay his impending death is no so sad that he can't push it aside from time to time. Wolitzer tells us that grief and loss need not be all-consuming. Life flourishes even in the little moments that are left, and in death there truly can be a living testament, the author is saying, for she celebrates life much more than death in this book.

Suppose... instead of one dying character we have two people on a terminal slide, and the book is about them and them alone? Suppose further that they are in love with one another...

This is the plot of Erich Maria Remarque's 1961 work, *Heaven Has No Favorites*, the story of a European race-car driver and a lovely young patient in a tuberculosis sanitarium. Clerfayt, the race-car driver, is over 40; Lillian, the patient, is in her twenties, and they fall in love simply and completely. Each day both of them face iminent death, yet neither wants to focus on the days when one or the other will no longer be there. Grief and loss? They try to ignore it in their mad dash towards oblivion. "Both of us have no future," Lillian thinks, "His reaches only to the next race, and mine to the next hemmorrhage."

Clerfayt convinces Lillian to leave her sanitarium, to join him in the exciting life he follows... hard drinking and danger, Paris, Sicily, Venice, champagne and fine wines, dinner in three-star restaurants, a permanent apartment at the Ritz, a villa on the Riviera... Lillian knows that her X-rays give her no more than a year to live, and Clerfayt assures her the months will be spent as if she is healthy, hearty and with a full future. Grief and loss? Only in the deepest portion of the mind and then only for the briefest instant. Is there fear of death? Yes, Remarque tells us, but it is a positive kind of feeling because only in the presence of death can we become most human and able to love. The fear of death induces the rise of love, and so whatever grief and sense of loss there may be is nothing more than a springboard to establish and validate love, love, love.

Suicide is a story spicer here, of course, not only with Lillian but with Clerfayt, as well. Lillian understands it better than he does because her outlook is inexorably written while his is still subject to personal choice. But from the beginning the choice has already been made for Clerfayt; he can no more give up racing than Lillian could give up her medicines. He is addicted to danger, and so his end is just as inexorable as Lillian's. There's a minor parallel between this story and Shakespeare's *Romeo and Juliet*, in that the love affair is doomed from the outset in both works. The protagonists expend their love in the face of impending death, and in some strange way they are all uplifted by it. Grief and loss? Felt perhaps by others, but the lovers themselves have little time to dwell on it.

So, we can have grief and loss as a plot motivator *even* if they are notable by their absence. The lovers reject the idea of loss and grief over their lot, they concern themselves with the present and the pleasure it can provide.

Remember, you must die!... Suppose we hear those words from an anonymous stranger over the telephone. Suppose we're over 70 years of age, we live with other septuagenarians in a home, and each one of us gets the same telephone message!

It's the central catalyst for a story that treats death and dying with a wry humor. Yes, there can be laughs in the midst of grief and loss; things don't have to be sticky and sad, page after page. Muriel Spark shows us how with her 1958 book, *Momento mori*, a tale of those in the last stages of life and their reactions to being reminded about it. This is not a House of Death book because there are no bedside vigils, no central dying figure. Instead, we have a housekeeper who runs a blackmail business among her housemates — an eighty-seven year old who retains a lubricious eye for the ladies and pays handsomely for the privilege of eyeing gartered female legs; a seventy-nine-year-old amateur gerontologist who gloats when he spies signs of further aging in others, records such signs compulsively and asks his housemates for their pulse rates.

Then come the phone calls. The police are consulted, but

they can find no answers. Reactions among the members of the home differ, from those who simply ignore the calls to those who are reminded to adjust their affairs and to purify their consciences. This is not a book that dwells on sadness and grief. Even facing the imminence of death, the characters maintain their foibles and follow their inclinations. Why should an eighty-seven-year-old not be allowed to ogle a pair of sexy legs? . . . or a seventy-nine-year-old be prevented from needling his contemporaries about their ages and their health? There is lightness here, and it helps to motivate the plot by showing the sunny side of grief and loss.

Is this plot stealable?

What if. . . we change the locale to an Air Force base in England during the Second World War with missions being flown day and night.

What if. . . we have a character who is in constant heat for the nurses, following them about the base, pursuing them for dates, touching, feeling, pinching, grabbing.

What if. . . we have a character using the Air Force to perpetuate his various schemes to get rich and buy his way out of the war.

What if. . . we have a character who keeps private, detailed records of deaths and injuries suffered by every section of the unit.

What if. . . periodically the members of the unit get black-edged cards with the inscription, ''Death is the only release!''

The institutional setting, the spectre of death, the bizarre reactions of those who must cope — all of this might have taken place in Joseph Heller's *Catch Twenty-Two*.

But it doesn't.

We've just used ''what if. . .'' to change things around a bit. Simple, really.

8

Rebellion

A rebellion is a... revolution is a... coup détat is an... insurrection. "If you've seen one, you've seen them all," a former vice-president of the United States once remarked. He was referring to an urban ghetto where minorities struggled, passing their days in abject poverty. But his remark — insensitive and inaccurate though it was — could be applied to situations where active challenge to established authority takes place. "If you've seen one challenge to authority, you've seen them all," may not be without exception, but stories which contain a strong dose of rebellion or coup détat or revolution or insurrection seem to follow similar lines.

There's authority being challenged, and most often it is a government or political entity rigidly enforcing its own standards or rules. But it doesn't have to be political. How about *One Flew Over the Cuckoo's Nest*, Ken Kesey's fine work about the challenge to authority in a mental institution? In a sense the mental institution is a separate state, at least to those who are confined behind its walls. Randall McMurphy, the protagonist, is the primary challenger to the institution's authority, and the challenge he makes is not so much to overthrow authority as to attempt to relax the rules. He ridicules, he teases, he creates mischief in order to demonstrate to Miss Ratched, the head nurse and his major adversary, that the rules are silly, pointless and in some instances downright dangerous. His rebellion is more of the spirit than for material gain, though he is obviously striving for some form of power.

And that's the next similarity about stories that use challenge to authority as a plot motivator. There's that search, that urge for power. We rebel to throw off someone else's yoke, but in doing it don't we also look to gain power? Take *The Caine Mutiny*, written in 1951 by Herman Wouk. It's the story of an aging minesweeper during the Second World War, her skipper's rapidly developing paranoia, the effect on the crew and the ultimate challenge. It's the saga of Willie Keith, a Princeton graduate who becomes a junior officer on the *S.S. Caine*, as the ship readies herself for sea duty in the South Pacific. Her new captain is Philip Queeg, a veteran of the battle of the Atlantic, tired now and worn. As Queeg begins to distrust every one of his officers and men and actually wonders whether there are plots to unseat him, Willie Keith and the other officers conspire to take command from him. They consider him dangerously unreliable, and they fear for their lives. And then, as *The Caine* wallows perilously in the fury of a typhoon, Queeg appears lost and confused, and his command is taken over on the spot. The challenge has succeeded, and in the ensuing court-martial the actions of the officers in taking away Queeg's command are ratified. Queeg's power over them has been stripped, and they are now free to develop their own destinies. They have acquired power for themselves.

In stories where rebellion and a challenge to authority become the plot motivator, there will usually be some aspect of survival, as well. Perhaps it might even be a co-plot motivator, but whether we're concerned about the one whose authority is being challenged or the one who is doing the challenging, the way either or both survive the challenge is most important. Surviving the rebellion... how it is done... what will replace the old order... are significant circumstances to write about. What does surviving do to the characters, to their relationships? What about those who don't survive?

Obviously, rebellion coupled with survival is fertile pickings for story spicers. Honor and dishonor are almost always there, as well as conspiracy and authority. In fact, it would be rare to find a story motivated by rebellion that didn't contain at least these four story spicers.

This is especially true when the setting is the political arena. "Man is a political animal," wrote Aristotle, and so political events become exciting, important and life-measuring. Challenging authority in the political sense is a frequent source for stories, and it presents an opportunity for an author to range over a wide setting.

For example, in Charles Dickens's *A Tale of Two Cities*, the author uses the French Revolution as a background for the political intrigues and love interests that are fostered both in London and Paris. In the courtroom of Old Bailey in London, Charles Darnay is on trial for treason for conducting secret business between France and England. Lucie Manette and her father, Dr. Manette, are there and have testified that five years earlier they had met Darnay on the boat from France to England. Then, Darnay's counsel turns and points at another man seated in the courtroom. He asks whether the identification could still be made. The other man, Sidney Carton, a hack lawyer and alcoholic, has a remarkable resemblance to Darnay. It is so strong, in fact, that the identification of Darnay is shaken and he is ultimately acquitted.

But in the aftermath both Darnay and Carton become attracted to Lucie Manette and become callers at the Manette household in London. At this same time the seeds of the Revolution in France are sprouting, and one day an aristocrat, the Marquis de St. Evremonde, is driving his carriage through the countryside and carelessly kills the innocent child of a peasant, Gaspard. Later the Marquis returns to his castle and meets his nephew, Charles Darnay, who is visiting from England. Darnay has heard about his uncle's accident, and knows about other skeletons in the family closet. He implores his uncle to make amends, but he is haughtily rebuffed. That night the Marquis is murdered in his bed.

Darnay then goes back to England and asks Dr. Manette if he may court Lucie and offers to give his real French name. Dr. Manette fends him off on the name, asking that he reveal it only on the morning of his marriage. At this same time Sidney Carton asks Lucie to marry him, but she refuses. He then tells her that he will is prepared to offer his own life for her at any time should the need ever arise.

In France, word has come that Lucie will marry Charles Darnay, and this upsets the revolutionists, particularly Madame Defarge and her husband, because Dr. Manette was a prisoner in the Bastille years before and is a hero to those challenging the monarchy. For his daughter to marry an aristocrat is unthinkable! Nevertheless, Darnay and Lucie are married, and Sidney Carton becomes a good family friend.

It's 1789 now and the revolution boils over. The Bastille is stormed, and in the ensuing chaos, Defarge goes to the cell where Dr. Manette was held and finds some papers hidden behind a stone in the wall. It is an account of Dr. Manette's arrest and imprisonment because he had discovered the crime of the Marquis de St. Evremonde against a poor, young woman and her brother. Defarge decides to hold the papers for possible future use.

In London Darnay receives a letter from an old family servant in France saying he is imprisoned and fears for his life. Would Darnay help him?

Darnay goes to France and shortly after he has arrived, he is arrested as an undesirable immigrant. Lucie and her father arrive, and the doctor feels that his own imprisonment in the Bastille years before will give him credence to plead for his son-in-law, even though he is an aristocrat. Fifteen months later Darnay is brought to trial and convinces the court (with the help of Dr. Manette) he is innocent of any crimes against the French people. He is released, but ordered to stay in France. Then, a little later, Darnay is rearrested, denounced by Defarge and by one other person Defarge refuses to divulge (who later turns out to be Madame Defarge).

At this time Sidney Carton arrives in France after hearing of the plight of his friends. He goes to Madame Defarge's wine shop where he discovers she is the sister of the woman the Marquis de St. Evremonde had raped many years before. He knows, then, that Darnay will not escape the guillotine, so he goes to the prison, drugs Darnay and with an accomplice has him taken from the cell. Then, because of his remarkable resemblance to Darnay, Carton takes his place in the cell. Meanwhile, Darnay and Lucie return safely to England, and Sidney Carton ultimately loses his life to the guillotine.

Dickens's book deals not so much with the preliminary stages of the French Revolution as with events following the start of the Revolution when new authority was attempting to solidify itself. Still, the question of power and the challenge to that power and authority are what are played out here. As a plot motivator the rebellion — in this case the Revolution — is central to the story line. Without the swirling events of the Revolution providing motive and reason for what the characters do, there really would be no story. Why is Charles Darnay arrested? Why is Madame Defarge bound for revenge on the St. Evremonde family? Why is Charles Darnay in Old Bailey and on trial early in the book?

These and other questions are the framework of the plot, but they motivate the plot only when they are woven into the tapestry of the French Revolution.

Story spicers abound here — authority, honor and dishonor, and conspiracy, of course. But there's mistaken identity, too, and deception and suspicion and criminal action. Because the story is painted against a broad background, it is not unlikely that a variety of story spicers would be present. They provide choices for the plot, and give it added dimension. The more story spicers there are, the more opportunities exist for subplots and extended action. We can imagine adding still more story spicers, using what if . . . to create a different story. How about unnatural affection? Suppose Sidney Carton and Charles Darnay have a homosexual relationship (hardly proper literature in Victorian England but certainly no problem today), and they try to keep their relationship quiet even as they both struggle with their feelings for Lucie and for one another. Or suppose Dr. Manette and Lucie have an erotic bond that interferes with the desires of both Darnay and Carton . . .

The drift is clear, of course. We can play what if . . . and we can make the plot come out any way we wish. The important thing to remember is that no story is locked in a steel box forever. Parts of it can always be used, or it can be changed in any direction. Changing just one story spicer might create a whole new story. The opportunities are boundless.

Did Dickens steal his plot? Probably not, though there are many stories of political cross-currents in the midst of a challenge to authority. In Shakespeare the question was always hanging there — is the new order any better than the old? *Macbeth, King Lear, Julius Ceasar*, among other Shakespearean dramas, show us that man's political motives are often narrow, self-concerned and not particularly benign. However, it doesn't always have to be that way. In the early 19th century Johann von Schiller wrote his famous *William Tell*, a story about a strong, silent hero who emerges from obscurity to rally a rebellion and then retreats back to obscurity. Schiller based the plot on a popular legend that grew out of the animosity between Austria and the Swiss in the fifteenth century. Schiller played what if... the Emperor of Austria sends his personal representative, Gessler, to rule over the forest cantons of Switzerland, and Gessler finds to his anger that the Swiss hold their lands in fief to the Emperor himself and not to his appointed representative. The prosperous, independent Swiss show Gessler to be a paper tiger with only limited authority over the citizens. Now, what if... Gessler determines to exert his own authority and mounts a cap on a pole in a public place, requiring that each man bow to it.

Then, Gessler goes even further and sends his own men to the farm of Henry of Halden, demanding he turn over his best team of oxen. Henry's son, Arnold, refuses, and attacks Gessler's men, driving them away. But Arnold realizes he had better go into hiding, and while he is away, Gessler's soldiers come back and torture Henry and put out his eyes.

So, what if... popular miscontent rises and Walter Furst, William Tell's father-in-law, becomes the leader of the free Switzerland movement. They meet in great secrecy and decide to revive their ancient parliament, though they delay the cry for a popular uprising until the Christmas season.

At this time William Tell and his sons walk past the pole with the cap on top, and really more by accident than design, pay no attention. Tell is immediately arrested, and his father-in-law pleads with the guards for his release. But William Tell submits to his captors, and as he is being led away Gessler rides by.

He spies Tell's son, Walter Tell, and has an apple placed on the youth's head. Use your bow, he commands Tell, and see if you can shoot the apple from your son's head.

Tell protests, but Gessler is adamant. "Do it!" he commands. So, Tell takes out two arrows and neatly fits one in his crossbow. He aims at the apple on Walter's head and splits it.

"Why did you take two arrows?" Gessler asks.

Tell refuses to answer until Gessler promises not to harm him, no matter what the answer.

Now, what if... Tell says that if his arrow had missed the apple and hurt his son, he would have shot the remaining arrow into Gessler. Gessler, angered by this impudence, forgets his pledge and has William Tell arrested on the spot. He decides to imprison Tell in his castle for life.

On the boat that will take them to Gessler's castle, William Tell is in chains. But a storm comes up and the boat is pitching furiously. What if... Gessler, in fear for his life, implores William Tell to save them, and he unbinds the chains. Tell takes over the helm and guides the boat close to shore where he leaps to safety, then disappears into the forest.

Later, he finds a path on which Gessler must travel to escape the fury of the storm. And he waits for the tyrant. While he is in hiding, a woman and her children come along, hoping to intercept Gessler and plead for clemency for their husband and father who is in prison for a minor offense. Finally, Gessler approaces with his hangers-on and many, many citizens. The woman stops him and makes her appeal for clemency. But Gessler denies the plea.

And that is all William Tell waits to hear. He sights, aims and shoots an arrow from his crossbow, hitting Gessler in the chest. He emerges from his hiding place and announces that it is he who has shot Gessler. Then, quick as he appears, he disappears back into the forest, leaving Gessler to bleed to death in front of so many he has oppressed. And in the ensuing period a free Switzerland is born.

Thus is hatched the modern legend of William Tell, the quiet, unassuming forester who is aroused to action only by the injustice of the tyrant. A bigger-than-life hero, really, someone we could imagine in graphic color depicted on the cover of *Zap*! comics or a modern reincarnation of the western movie tyro, Shane. The hero who does his heroics for the betterment of mankind and not for any personal glory or reward.

Clearly, Schiller stole his plot here. There's no question the William Tell story came from a centuries-old legend, and even if Schiller stayed close to the truth of the legend, the story line did not come from thin air. In fact, Schiller admitted that he went into the old Swiss Chronicles and discovered the apple-shooting sequence, though not too much else. There were many loose threads — partial story ideas, characters and events, but they weren't tied together in any sort of frame. He had to do that himself. Still, if he hadn't found the incident of William Tell shooting the apple from his son's head, there might not be a modern *William Tell* today.

And we wouldn't see still another example of an author stealing a plot — and admitting it!

Now, let's take what if. . . a step still further. Let's look at a current explosive political situation and turn it around. Let's ask what if. . . there has already been an uprising in South Africa, the blacks have taken over the country and the whites are in fear for their lives. Nadine Gordimer spins this tale in her 1981 book, *July's People*. Here, the rebellion is in full swing, the cities are under siege, the suburbs are in smoke, vigilante groups roam the streets. The central characters are Maureen and Bam Smales, and they, along with their three children, are face-to-face with what is happening. Then their black houseservant, July, offers to guide them to safety at his home village in the bush. They snap at the chance, and the Smaleses, under the protective custody of July, make the trek to an all-black village miles, physically and culturally, from their accustomed affluence and conveniences. The village consists of mud huts with thatched roofs, and slowly, as the Smaleses settle in, they begin to run out of the paraphernalia of civilization they had brought with them — canned sausages, toilet paper, pills. They become totally dependent on July for their survival, never really recognizing that in helping them, he is also betraying his own people.

Obviously, there are political and socio-economic overtones in this book. Gordimer shows us how it might be if the tables are turned, and we have to fit ourselves within an alien culture. She plays what if... with an unerring eye for the ironies that make us realize how fragile our existences can be. Survival, of course, plays a strong part here because we are caught up in the way the Smaleses cope with their changed circumstances. But it is the overthrow of the old order — the black-led rebellion — that moves the story along. Without it, somehow, we'd be asking, why in the world would people *want* to live this way?

The nature of stories that use rebellion (or revolution, insurrection, coup détat) as plot motivator is that there has to be action, often violent action. Rebellion, by its very nature, implies challenge, conflict, some form of resistance. Action — and reaction — build the story, even though we may be dealing with something other than political events. The rebellion of a young child against its parents, for instance... or the rebellion of employees against an unreasonable employer... or the rebellion of a husband (or wife) against the other spouse... anything, in other words, that creates a challenge and demands some type of redress. "Every revolution was first a thought in one man's mind," wrote Ralph Waldo Emerson many years ago. If we remember that, then rebellion as a plot motivator can be seen in its simplest form. It is just a *way* of telling a story.

9

Betrayal

Suppose we have a character who is to do something, take some action, be somewhere; others rely upon him, and he knows it. If he deliberately ignores what he's supposed to do, and this brings harm or suffering to anyone, we have the essence of a story. If we start painting in the corners and filling in the spaces, we can label the story as one of betrayal. He has betrayed those who have relied upon him.

Betrayal... treachery... deception... cheating... all of these and more are what has happened, and when we dig a little bit, we're almost certain to have a good story, because stories of betrayal bring out the rawest emotions and precipitate the strongest reactions. It's natural. If we place our trust in someone or rely on them and they *deliberately* take advantage of that to gain something for themselves and we suffer directly for it, the seeds of vengeance are going to sprout in a hurry.

It happens in real life all too often. Betrayal and vengeance go hand-in-hand, one bringing the other out, in a circle of disillusionment and hate that sparks violence and death. Somehow when we're betrayed, it's different from being attacked without provocation. It's worse because we've seen our faith and trust not only slammed back in our faces but hurt us as well. We're victims in a special way because we've allowed ourselves to be deluded.

So, stories of betrayal carry many possibilities, but it all comes down to one basic situation: a person who has put trust in another, has that trust shattered. The result can be a dynamic tale.

There's no better example of this than in *Agamemnon*, the first play of the famous trilogy, *The House of Atrius*, by the Greek playwright, Asschylus. This is a story of betrayal at the dawn of civilization, and all stories of betrayal that come after must acknowledge this great drama as setting the standard.

Taken together, the trilogy *The House of Atrius* is more a tale of vengeance than betrayal, but in the first play, *Agamemnon*, it is betrayal that is highlighted.

The story begins, as do so many of the Greek dramas, with the events of the Trojan War. Agamemnon and Menelaus are brothers, and it is the abduction of Helen, Menelaus's wife, by Paris, which leads to the war. Agamemnon offers to help his brother get Helen back, and off they go to battle. But on the way to Troy, Agamemnon becomes convinced that the Gods want him to sacrifice his daughter, Iphigenia, and so he does, much to the horror of his wife, Clytemnestra, who vows revenge.

While Agamemnon is away fighting, Clytemnestra is joined in her anger by Aegisthus, whose brothers and sisters had been murdered by Agamemnon's father, Atrius, and their flesh served at a royal banquet to their father. As Clytemnestra and Aegisthus nurse their common hate, they plot against Agamemnon and then become lovers.

So, Agamemnon returns victorious from Troy, and arrives at his palace by chariot. He has left his men quartered in town and is accompanied only by the young, attractive Cassandra, daughter of the King of Troy. She has fallen to him as his share of the spoils, and, of course, they also have become lovers.

Clytemnestra greets Agamemnon warmly, at the palace doorway, insisting that the royal carpet be placed for him to tread upon. Agamemnon asks Clytemnestra to receive Cassandra without bitterness, and then he goes into the palace to refresh himself.

Clytemnestra orders Cassandra into the palace, but she refuses and remains in the chariot. Furious, Clytemnestra storms off. "I will not make myself base by wasting words on her," she vows.

Then Cassandra gets out of the chariot and implores the gods to tell why she had been brought to this cursed house. And she prophesies what is about to happen...

> Ha! woman wilt thou dare?
> Thy bed's partner and thy mate
> In the warm refreshing bath
> Shall he find his bloody fate?...
> She strikes! and in the water
> Of the bath he falls. Mark well,
> In the bath doth murder dwell.

Then, she further prophesies her own death, and she goes inside the palace to meet her fate.

A few moments later Clytemnestra appears with the bloody sword of Aegisthus in her hand. She has killed both Agamemnon and Cassandra, and she implores the citizens gathered outside the palace to understand her motives. Agamemnon has killed her daughter, Iphigenia, he has shamed Clytemnestra by bringing Cassandra to the palace...

> What I did, I did
> Not from a random inconsiderate blow,
> But from old Hate, and with maturing Time...

Here lieth he that wronged a much-wronged woman...
And for this spear-won maid, this prophetess,
This wise diviner, will-beloved bed-fellow,
And trusted messmate of great Agamemnon,
She shares his fate, paying with him the fee
Of her own sin, and like a swan hath sung
Her mortal song beside him. She hath been
Rare seasoning added to my banquet fare.

Then she introduces Aegisthus who claims he will rule in Agamemnon's place. But the citizens don't want this. Clytemnestra and Aegisthus reject the criticism, even though there are cries that Orestes, the son of Agamemnon, would return from his exile and avenge his father's murder.

But Clytemnestra and Aegisthus turn a deaf ear to all this. "Heed not thou these brainless barkings," Clytemnestra reassures Aegisthus. We will convince the citizens that what we have done is right.

In the second part of the trilogy, *The Libation Bearers*, Orestes becomes aware of the murder of his father, and after a period of mourning vows vengeance on his mother and Aegisthus. He is joined in all of this by his sister, Electra, whom he meets at his father's tomb and with whom he plots the murder of his mother and her lover. In disguise he goes to Argos where he kills Aegisthus first and then Clytemnestra...

Betrayal and vengeance work hand-in-hand throughout this work. Clytemnestra hates Agamemnon because he has sacrificed their daughter. She feels betrayed by his blood-letting; she feels further betrayed by his returning to the palace with Cassandra; Orestes feels betrayed because his mother has killed his father and has done so with her lover whom she is now actively supporting. How do these feelings of betrayal become mobilized into action? By the swearing of vengeance, by a demand that someone answer for the acts of betrayal.

If someone deliberately ignores a responsibility and it brings harm or suffering, there has been a betrayal. In *Agamemnon* it is, of course, Agamemnon's responsibility to see to the safety of his daughter, Iphigenia (instead, he has her sacrificed), and to remain true to his wife, Clytemnestra (instead, he flaunts his relationship with Cassandra).

So, where the plot motivator, betrayal, is present, the co-plot motivator, vengeance, is also likely to appear. One seems to complement the other.

And could we steal the plot of *Agamemnon* or *The House of Atrius*?

It's easy. Many have done it. One of the latest is Joyce Carol Oates in her 1981 novel, *Angel of Light*. Maurice Halleck is a high federal official, director of the Commission for the Ministry of Justice. There is a scandal and Halleck is accused of taking a bribe so a multi-national corporation can continue its illegal activities in South America. Halleck is forced from office, and in disgrace he allegedly commits suicide.

His wife, Isabel, has been having an affair with Nick Martens, an old friend of Halleck's, and in fact Martens eventually succeeds to the post Halleck occupied. In flashbacks the author shows that the relationship of Halleck and Martens goes back more than 30 years, and that when they were both young, Martens actually saved Halleck's life. This brought such gratitude from Halleck's family that Martens's education and career were insured.

At this point, enter Halleck's two children, Kirsten, young, drug-dependent, boarding school educated, anorexic and emotionally unstable, and Owen, a dull, thick-witted Princetonian with an urge to succeed in corporate America. Kirsten is convinced Halleck was murdered by Isabel and Martens, and slowly she convinces Owen. Their mother has betrayed them and their father. They must seek vengeance...

And here we have the plot of *The House of Atrius*, refined and updated. Mother and lover kill husband... lover takes husband's place... children find out... children plot to kill mother and lover.

In refining her plot, Oates brings in a group of terrorists who believe that perhaps Kirsten and Owen have a point about who murdered their father and that it was done for political purposes. Owen, in fact, is killed in a terrorist bombing of his house after he has killed his mother. But this is done simply to keep things current, and it doesn't deflect the basic story line.

What about story spicers here? There's conspiracy (mother and lover conspiring to kill father and husband), deception (mother and lover keeping their affair quiet), criminal action (murder, murder, murder), suicide (Halleck's alleged death), honor and dishonor (the memory and reputation of father). Note how important a story spicer like deception becomes. The plot is motivated by betrayal, but it becomes all the more significant when the wife and the lover conceal their affair in the hope of succeeding to the power held by the husband. The deception hides the betrayal and provides still another motive for vengeance... *They tried to keep it from us!* the children say... *they knew they couldn't have achieved what they wanted if they didn't hide the affair!* The act of deception is a betrayal in that it allows the mother and her lover to ignore their responsibilities to the father and to the children.

When we think of betrayal, mostly we consider it in terms of the eternal love triangle — husband, wife, lover. That is certainly one aspect in *The House of Atrius* and *Angel of Light*, though, of course, there were other involvements as well. Yet the love triangle can also be the central core of a story and provide the full measure of motivations for all the action. Such is the case with a 1968 novel by Vladimir Nabokov, *King, Queen, Knave*. The story is set in Berlin in 1928, and the main characters are Dreyer, a wealthy, over-friendly department-store owner, his bored, materialistic wife, Martha, and Franz, Dreyer's country-bumpkin nephew. The story opens as Dreyer and Martha are returning from vacation; they are traveling by train, and into their compartment comes Franz, unknown to them both. Though no words are exchanged, Dreyer can't help turning up his nose at Franz, thinking him the essence of clumsy oafishness. But then, later, Franz arrives at Dreyer's home, introducing himself and asking for a job. So Dreyer hires him and allows him to stay in the rich, lavishly furnished home. Gradually, Martha and Franz get it on, Martha surprising herself by her feelings for someone she seemingly has so little in common with. As the casual affair heats into a grand passion, Martha and Franz begin to covet Dreyer's fortune. Martha especially... "My dining room, my earrings, my silver, my Franz..." In her boredom and slow slide into degradation, Martha has been painted by Nabokov in the image of Flaubert's *Madame Bovary*, someone who is dissatisfied with her lot and forever looking for something or someone to take her out of it, but of course, with Martha, as with Emma Bovary, the white knight is hardly up to the task. Here, Martha and Franz finally hatch a plot — they will kill Dreyer and then have his fortune. But Martha is doomed by her own greed. Even as she is about to kill Dreyer, he informs her that his net worth will jump one hundred thousand dollars from the proceeds of a mechanical mannequin patent...

Martha hesitates, and the thought of all that extra money is just too much for her. She aborts the murder attempt, but it is too late. She has caught pneumonia in the attempt and slowly expires.

And Franz? In the grand tradition of the Greek dramas, he is so bereft by her loss and by his other confusions that he goes mad.

And Dreyer? As the one betrayed, he has had his vengeance, even though he doesn't know it.

All of this seems to say betrayal sparks stories which convey only anger and serious, heavy emotion — that a tale of betrayal can't have its light, funny moments. Not so, of course. But when we think of betrayal, we tend to equate it with treachery, and there really can't be much humor in that! Yet the eternal love triangle can be couched to keep us laughing, provided, of course, that we stay away from story spicers such as criminal action (murder, murder, murder!) and suicide. Nora Ephron accomplishes this in a 1983 book, *Heartburn*, her story of Rachael Samstad, a cookbook author and former television personality who is seven and one-half months pregnant when she discovers that her husband has been having an affair with the wife of the Under Secretary of State for Middle Eastern Affairs. Rachael and the story move back and forth between Washington and New York as the birth of her baby draws closer and she tries to come to terms with what is happening. Her husband, Mark Feldman, is a syndicated columnist, and he becomes the foil for much of the humor. "The man is capable of having sex with a venetian blind..." Ephron writes. And when Mark suddenly becomes contrite and uncharacteristically bursts into tears, "It's true that men who cry are sensitive to and in touch with their feelings, but the only feelings they tend to be sensitive to and in touch with are their own..." She paints the characters in burlesque hues: Jonathon Rice, for example, husband of Mark's lady friend, spends his time hiding in the shrubbery with earphones, eavesdropping on the conniving pair. And she is constantly casting an amusing light on herself: "The most unfair thing about this whole business is that I can't even date..."

But underneath the humor is the fact of the betrayal, and, of course, Rachael wants some sort of vengeance. To soothe her shattered feelings, she produces recipes which are spread throughout the book. These recipes are a form of sanity for her, a touch of reality in her crumbling world. There is a time when Mark wants to return to her, but she'll have none of that! In the end, Rachael Samstad, cookbook author, mother and single parent, faces the world a bit wiser but no less scarred from being betrayed.

Shakespeare dealt with betrayal in the eternal love triangle, though certainly not humorously. But in this case it is a story of *imagined* betrayal which leads to sorrowful consequences. In truth there has been no betrayal, but events transpire on the basis that a betrayal has supposedly occurred. *Othello* is the play, and the story shows that betrayal can motivate a plot even though it doesn't actually take place. The important thing to remember is what the characters think goes on — their suspicions, their false assumptions.

In the story Othello, a Moor and a general in the Venetian army, falls in love with and secretly marries Desdemona, daughter of Brabantio, a Venetian senator. Othello picks Cassio instead of Iago as his lieutenant and Iago vows vengeance for the slight.

Then the Turks attack Cyprus, and Othello is dispatched to take charge of the defense. Iago, nursing his anger, proceeds to get Cassio drunk while on duty, and this causes Cassio's demotion. Desdemona, meanwhile, has joined Othello with the army, and Iago subtly implants the idea in Othello's head that Desdemona and Cassio have been having an affair. Although he resists mightily, Othello's suspicions slowly become aroused. Cassio, of course, is chagrined at what happened to him, and he seeks advice from Iago about how to regain his rank. Have Desdemona plead your case, Iago advises him. She knows you, she will sway the general.

What it does — as Iago hoped — is to arouse Othello's suspicions even further. Then, to tighten the noose, Iago plants a handkerchief on Cassio that Othello has given to Desdemona. This convinces Othello that Desdemona has betrayed him with Cassio. Late at night he enters the bedchamber he and Desdemona share. She is asleep. Othello stares at her, sure now that he must kill her. . .

> Yet I'll not shed her blood;
> Nor scar that whiter skin of hers than show,
> And smooth as monumental alabaster.

Yet she must die, else she'll betray more men...

And he smothers her with a pillow. Subsequently, Iago's plotting is uncovered, and he is arrested. Othello tries to kill him but fails. In despair he then kills himself.

And the betrayal, which is nothing more than a seed planted in Othello's mind by a revenge-bent Iago (again, betrayal and vengeance working together), has claimed its victims. As Shakespeare sees clearly, betrayal can be just as effective as a plot motivator even if it actually never occurs. What the mind thinks is the clearest reality, and this is more than enough for an effective story line.

Stories of betrayal can blossom in settings far removed from the eternal love triangle. In fact, when we think of betrayal's alter ego — treachery — politics and espionage are relevant, for here we can have betrayal on a grand scale. What if... a U.S. Ambassador is blackmailed by the enemy? What if... a group of terrorists get their hands on a nuclear bomb through the misguided actions of a high-level scientists? What if... the secrets of a vital U.S. defense position are stolen? What if... someone entrusted to guard the person of the president of the United States is secretly planning to kill him?

All of these story lines have been used before, and yet they represent only a slice of the plots available with betrayal as a motivator. Politics calls up an urge for power, and success can bring a heady victory. The rewards can be substantial, and that is why a character — or characters — can rationalize that the ends (political power) can justify the means (betrayal). Such is the ambition of a murderous, sadistic young man portrayed by Dan Jacobson in his 1977 book *The Confessions of Josef Baisz*. Baisz is born to a working class family in the imaginary republic of Sarmeda (patterned to an extent on Jacobsen's native South Africa). The story is actually a manuscript purporting to be the final confession of Baisz, his earthly testament, so to speak, of crimes committed during a lifetime as an informer, treacherous bodyguard, murderer and police spy. After his father commits suicide, Baisz decides "to do better than my father, to know more about others than they know about me."

And he begins his slow climb up the ladder of betrayal, first as an informer on his best friend, then as a member of the secret police where he follows orders and kidnaps two young children, then as the protector of a young man whom he proceeds to murder. He ends up betraying his sister and finally decides to commit suicide, becoming, himself, the most justifiable of all of his victims.

The line of betrayal in this work is unrelenting, and Baisz succeeds in making use of various forms of it in his search for power and security. Jacobson paints him as absolutely amoral, and in politics this may be the most appropriate way to be. The point is that the betrayals of Josef Baisz are accomplished without high-mindedness or lofty ideals (compare George Smiley in some of John Le Carre's stories — a spy to be sure but, somehow, whatever is to be done is dusted with the certainty that man's last, best hope remains the preservation of English society). Baisz's betrayals are nothing more than means to serve the ends of his own rising importance. Story spicers such as deception, conspiracy, criminal action and authority make their appearances, but the plot is essentially a fanfare of betrayal. The plot motivator *is* the story line in this instance, and of course the reader will feel revulsion at the doings in the story.

And that is the point, really. The reader will *feel*. . . something! The plot is certainly there for the taking.

Josef Baisz admits his betrayal baldly. An equally intriguing story line might have been whether, in fact, he betrayed for his own sake or in the name of his country. Was there political treachery and, if so, by whom? It is a popular framework for a story because it adds suspense to the question of the nature of the betrayal.

This is what Piers Paul Read does with *The Villa Golitsyn*, his

1981 book about the search for the betrayer of an English officer and his men in the undeclared war between Indonesia and Malaya in the 1960s. The Foreign Office has suspicions it is Willy Ludley, a member of the embassy staff during that period and now retired and living in the South of France on a comfortable family fortune. Simon Milson is sent by the Foreign Office to The Villa Golitsyn, Ludley's home, to ferret out the facts, and the bulk of the action takes place here. (There is a similarity to Agatha Christie's *Ten Little Indians* in that the search for the criminal takes place within the confines of an isolated mansion, the characters and their motivations are spelled out, their interaction is scrutinized and clues and blind alleys abound.) There is Priss, Ludley's wife who is a tease, Helen, a young girl who arrives unexpectedly at the Villa, Milson, himself, searching for an answer.

Questions about Ludley hover over the pages. Why does he drink so much? Why did he flee Jakarta so rapidly after the torture-killing of the officer and his men? Why has he lived in semi-isolation for more than twenty years?

These questions and more keep the story going. But the underlying theme is the motivation for seeking answers to the betrayal, and this is the essence of the book. If we were going to steal this plot, wouldn't we like to follow a theme which provides that the Foreign Office is "always afraid that the ideological bacillus which had raged through Cambridge in the 1930s might have infected later generations."

Did the betrayal occur, or didn't it?

That is the question!

10

Persecution

"Of all the tyrannies on human kind, the worst is that which persecutes the mind," wrote British poet John Dryden more than three hundred years ago. Persecution is that unfairest of all agonies because it is opposition raised to vicious, uncompromising harrassment. it is contentiousness on a scale that allows little in the way of mercy, understanding or approval. One is persecuted because one is different, and the very nature of persecution carries along deep-seated conflict and tension — the very elements that go into the making of a good story.

Persecution is made of more than just opposition. It is based on a distinction in social level or religion or origin — items which go far beyond a simple intellectual dispute because persecution usually ends in severe personal harm or death.

Persecution can be made most vivid when it is accomplished in the name of or directed at a single individual (even with the pervasive effects of the Holocaust as background, books such as *Sophie's Choice* by William Styron, *The Diary of Ann Frank*, and *QB VII* by Leon Uris remain the story of one person). "Opposition may become sweet to a man when he has christened it persecution," wrote George Eliot in the nineteenth century, and that's certainly true. If we're harrassed and opposed, and we know our lives are on the line, we call it persecution and somehow the battle seems more just, more right. For the persecutor the battle may seem equally just, but the bottom line is that both persecutor and the one being persecuted see their conflict as a struggle over basic, innate characteristics which, if left alone, would finally overwhelm and defeat the other.

Persecution is a powerful plot motivator, and it has formed the basis for many, many stories. Shakespeare recognizes the device and uses it in *Richard III*, his tragedy of the hunchbacked member of the House of York who persecuted all those standing in his way to the throne of England. Richard, to be sure, is the villain in this story, and through his conniving and treachery, lies and deceits he gains the throne. But the plot fairly bursts with his persecution of friends and relatives alike.

The story opens with Richard announcing his intent to play upon the suspicions of King Edward that under an old prophecy the King's issue would be disinherited by one of his heirs whose name begins with the letter "G" — a clear reference to Richard's brother, George, the Duke of Clarence. George is arrested, thrown in the Town of London where Richard, promising to free him, murders him instead.

This is but one in a string of murders that Richard conceives and carries out all in pursuit of the throne after King Edward dies. Along the way he stabs a deposed King (Henry VI) and his son, the Prince of Wales. He eliminates a variety of noblemen and followers, his own wife, the two young princes residing in the Tower who are in the direct line for the Crown and finally his own ally, Buckingham. In each instance, Richard senses a threat that can only be neutralized by doing away with the individual. Sometimes he is quite subtle about his scheming, as in the manner in which he is finally crowned... Buckingham, his ally, is told to emphasize at a meeting at the Guildhall that the late King Edward (whom Richard did *not* kill) had illegitimate children and was, himself, a bastard. He should imply that the late King's line was flawed and that Richard, whose family had impeccable royal credentials, should assume the throne.

The big lie works well enough so that the Lord Mayor and the citizens of London decide to offer Richard the crown. Buckingham suggests that he appear on a balcony with two bishops and seem to be deeply absorbed in a prayer book, affecting a strong sense of piety. Play hard to get, Buckingham suggests...

> *Mayor*
>
> Do, good my lord, your citizens entreat you.
>
> *Buckingham*
>
> Refuse not, mighty lord, this proffer'd love
>
> *Catesby*
>
> O, make them joyful, grant their lawful suit!
>
> *Richard*
>
> Alas, why would you heap these cares on me?
>
> I am unfit for state and majesty
>
> I do beseech you, take it not amiss
>
> I cannot nor will I yield to you...

But of course he does give in and he is crowned. Then, noting that the little princes are in the Tower, he fears for the security of his reign. He summons James Tyrrel (referred to as a "discontented gentleman") after Buckingham has parried a request to kill the little princes. Tyrrel agrees to do it, and goes to the Tower and smothers them as they lie sleeping in one another's arms. The agony of the moment is captured in Tyrrel's words:

> The tyrannous and bloody deed is done,
>
> The most arch act of piteous massacre
>
> That ever yet this land was guilty of...

Richard is finally forced to fight for his throne with Henry

Tudor who has been in exile in France and raising an army. They meet on Bosworth field, and the night before the final battle the ghosts of all those whom Richard has killed haunt his dreams, appearing one by one to condemn him.

Here, then, is a plot filled with the persecution of any who stood in Richard's way for the throne. In many ways it is just an updating of some of the old Greek tragedies where the number of bodies strewn about almost exceeds the cast of characters. But the theme is a viable one: opposition seen as so threatening that persecution must follow.

Did Shakespeare create this story? No. Scholars tell of a similar tale, the play *Richard Tertius*, in Dr. Legge's Latin chronicles. And then there is *Richard Crookback*, authored by Ben Jonson some years earlier.

What, then, is there to steal? If we update *Richard the Third*, we can see a modern equivalent in Mario Puzo's *The Godfather* where an undisputed leader persecutes his enemies (real or imagined) unmercifully. There is killing and treachery on a scale to rival *Richard the Third*, and while there is nothing to match the execution of the little princes, how about the artfully contrived simultaneous ambush slayings of the Barzini crime family? The plot motivator in both instances is persecution of enemies based on deep, fundamental differences.

What about a story spicer in *Richard the Third*? As befits a complicated plot there are several here. Perhaps the most significant is the resort to criminal action — specifically murder or murders — to achieve the necessary ends. If Richard had, somehow, attempted to outmaneuver those he felt opposed him, without giving in to murder, think how less effective and substantial the plot would have been. In fact, it would be little more than an innocuous history lesson. Also, of course, it probably wouldn't have been very realistic, given the tenor of the times approximately five hundred years ago. People *did* kill people to be crowned king. People even killed women and defenseless children. So, any plot dealing with the story of *Richard the Third* requires murder and treachery to make it real.

Shakespeare uses other story spicers as well. There is conspiracy in that Richard employs both Buckingham and Catesby to further his scheme and help him persecute his enemies. It is no less a conspiracy though Buckingham and Catesby are part of his retinue and owe him allegiance. The conspiracy is in agreeing to perform some illegal act together, and murder is certainly an illegal act.

Then, there is deception. Quite obviously, Richard deceived the Lord Mayor and the citizens of London by feigning indifference for the Crown. And there is the way he manipulated the suspicion of King Edward so that Richard's brother, George, would be tossed into the Tower, and there is his reassurance to George that he intends to free him — only to murder him instead. ·Deception, deception — it bursts from *Richard the Third*, but only to spice the underlying persecution. It cannot hold the story by itself.

Persecution as a plot motivator is equally effective when it can be portrayed through the eyes of the one being persecuted as through the eyes of the one doing the persecuting. In Nathaniel Hawthorne's *The Scarlet Letter*, written in 1850, we agonize with Hester Prynne in the early days of the Massachusetts Bay Colony as she is convicted of adultery and forced to stand in the public pillory holding and acknowledging her illigitimate child. The good citizens of puritan Boston have forced her to wear a red letter "A" embroidered on her breast to signify to one and all that she is an adulteress. The young minister, Arthur Dimmesdale, urges her to reveal the name of her lover, but she steadfastly refuses, and while she is in the pillory, her husband, Master Prynne, an English physician, arrives from Antwerp, Belgium and comes upon the scene. He has not laid eyes on her for two years because he had sent her on ahead to Boston. When he married her, she was very young, and from the beginning it had been a loveless marriage. Though the minister, Dimmesdale, continues urging Hester to divulge the name of her lover, he can't bring himself to admit, publicly or privately, that it is he.

In the meantime, Master Prynne determines to find out who impregnated his wife. He assumes a false name and succeeds in becoming Dimmesdale's doctor. His suspicions of Dimmesdale lead him to inflict various forms of mental anguish on the minister, including the implication that a scarlet letter is now burned into his flesh. Finally Dimmesdale can withhold the information no longer, and he joins Hester in the pillory where he publicly confesses to being her lover and the father of her child. The same day, he dies in Hester's arms.

The persecution of Hester by her puritan New England world provides a tale rich in social commentary and moral judgment. The plot is not complicated — a woman bearing an illigitimate child in early America — but the manner in which she is treated by her friends, neighbors, family and lover is what motivates the plot. Her persecution is symbolic for anyone's persecution when they defy the dictates of a religious and moral norm, and in showing this the author highlights the sheer ferocity of popular reaction.

Hawthorne's story is about the universality of sin, and in this sense there probably isn't a piece of work anywhere that doesn't touch on the issue. In a more specific way, too, the persecution of someone for flaunting moral values is a theme that has been picked up again and again. How about *Lady Chatterly's Lover*, written in 1928 by D.H. Lawrence? A titled English lady falls in love with her husband's gamekeeper, and they conduct a torrid affair under the nose of the husband. The language is rich in sexual detail and imagery, but an equally important aspect of the book is that what's going on violates the moral, cultural norm. It simply isn't done in upper-crust England in the nineteen twenties to get it on with the local gamekeeper. So, after agonizing about alternatives, the couple know there is only one choice — they must leave England forever, if they wish to remain together. It is the threat of persecution for their actions that motivates the plot here, and in the course of the book, Lawrence takes dead aim on a society that would treat others so viciously for partaking of simple sexual pleasure. In a broad sense, Lawrence *did* steal Hawthorne's plot, but he concentrated not on the aftereffects of the sexual activity but on the activity itself, detailing the persecution as threatened rather than already experienced.

Are there story spicers in Hawthorne's and Lawrence's work? Clearly, an item which provides solid substance throughout is the idea of authority. What is going on in both stories is that traditional authority is being ignored and the characters are pursuing their own personal gratifications. In puritan America it is the authority of the church and the community, and in the twentieth century in England it is the authority of the family and the traditional class system. The use of authority or the reaction to its use is a strong story spicer because it implies a good guys-bad guys theme — you're either for us or you're against us! Story conflicts like these make for good plots.

A fertile source of persecution drama has been the black-white racial conflict. Persecution and authority again come together here, and it's a framework that goes back hundreds of years. See, for example, *Uncle Tom's Cabin* by Harriet Beecher Stowe which was published in 1851 and its modern equivalent, Richard Wright's *Native Son*, a story of mob violence against the black man. It is persecution, not for strongly held beliefs or principles, but because of skin color, though of course a black skin carried certain innate expectations to the white man, and if they weren't fulfilled, the black man paid dearly.

On an individual level the story of one person's persecution can be a lesson for us all. In Harper Lee's *To Kill a Mockingbird*, written in 1960, the persecution is actually double-edged, affecting a black man and a white man. In a drowsy Alabama town sometime during the nineteen thirties, Atticus Finch, a widowed lawyer and the father of the narrator, Scout Finch, a young girl seven or eight years old, is assigned by the court to defend a black man, Tom Robinson, who is accused of raping a nineteen-year-old white girl. Though there are other themes in the book, persecution is what motivates the story because without it this would simply be a series of recollections about rural Alabama that could be found in the history books. But the author has used persecution to paint a vivid picture of southern life before the onset of the war. She has employed a classic device to build tension and conflict — a trial.

Atticus Finch, once named as Tom Robinson's counsel, sets to investigate the facts and discovers that he believes Tom to be innocent. The fact that a black man is going to stand trial for allegedly raping a white girl in the South in the nineteen thirties and that he will be judged by other white men is a form of persecution with which we are now all too familiar. Even Atticus Finch acknowledges that his client has probably been prejudged and will be found guilty. But he persists with a vigorous defense, and for that he is severely judged by his friends and neighbors. The family of the girl also attempt their own form of retribution, even threatening Atticus and Scout with physical harm. This is a family of poor, ignorant whites, who live off the refuse in the town dump and wait each month for their relief checks. They would love nothing better than to bring down a respected member of the community, to brand him as a "nigger lover."

But in the case of Atticus, at least, the persecution is of fairly short duration, and at the end of the book he is reelected to the state legislature. The question of Tom Robinson's fate is not so nicely disposed of, except that we see the fruits of persecution in bold relief. The black man is still not free, he is still the object of bias and bigotry even when his accuser is a white girl from a disreputable family. At least, Atticus tells Scout, since the jury took so long to decide Tom Robinson's fate (he is convicted), it indicates some progress toward erasing the stigma of being black in a white man's courtroom. Small consolation, though, to Tom Robinson.

Let's steal Harper Lee's plot — a lawyer defending an unpopular defendent and becoming the object of persecution and threats. What if... a social worker storms through the inertia-laden welfare system on behalf of a severely distressed client who happens to be both unpopular and unattractive?... or a doctor goes against conventional medical wisdom in order to uncover a new drug or to heal an especially unpopular patient?

If we stay with Harper Lee's plot, the story will involve someone with professional credentials, though, of course, the protagonist can be anyone practicing any trade. The point is to challenge the norm sufficiently to create a reaction so severe it becomes persecution. Then, we add a story spicer or two, and we have a complete story line.

On a broader scale the persecution inherent in the black-white conflict is portrayed by Nadine Gordimer in her 1981 novel, *Burgher's Daughter*. Here we have an entire national setting — South Africa and its appartheid policies — for the events and the reactions. But, just as Harper Lee's book shows, it comes down to the story of one person, or one family, against a background of racial persecution.

In this case, however, the family is white, and they are persecuted for their support and work with the black-liberation movement. Early in the book, Lionel Burgher, the father, a physician and Communist, dies in prison to which he has been sentenced because of his efforts for the black majority. His daughter, Rosa, is now the object of government surveillance and in order to survive she must live a life of secrecy and deception. Because of her constant concern for who is watching or listening, she moves through life like some carefully programmed robot, always aware of what effect her actions will have on others, not free to be spontaneous or carefree. But she harbors doubts about her dedication to the black movement and would like to travel abroad. Only the government won't permit it, requiring her to remain in South Africa.

She persists, however, and after much effort she finally gains a one-year travel permit on condition she stay away from anyone the South African government feels has anti-government attitudes. As she travels she finally finds the free expression and spontaneity she lacked before, and she has a fulfilling love affair with a Frenchman who provides her with a greater sense of herself.

But in the end she returns to South Africa to take up her father's work. And in the final pages she, herself, is now in jail becoming again the remote, carefully controlled person she was before. The apartheid dilemma is once again played out as a vivid mix of inhumanity and survival.

The persecution suffered by the Burgher family is the prime plot motivator, for without it, the political discord is little more than a mild debate and the suffering of the characters clearly unmotivated. Once again, authority is an ever-present story spicer since the persecution emanates directly from this source. Suspicion is also present, as are honor and dishonor since, after all, it is the dignity of the individual that this book is about. We honor that dignity or we dishonor it, by our treatment, and for Nadine Gordimer, honor wins out.

In persecution we have a plot motivator that can cut across economic, social and political lines. Its power is that of high emotion and the fulfillment of some overriding purpose. Evil or just, the elements of persecution call forth vivid action and a continuous testing of one's principles and goals.

Persecution propels a story with the force of the moral equation it always poses: is persecution ever justified and if so, when?

11

Self-Sacrifice

The young woman's eyes are bright with grief and determination. Her brother is dead, and he must be buried. Her sister stands with her in the early morning glow, and the sister isn't sure she wants to bury their brother.

I *will* bury him, the young woman says.

But the King has forbidden that he be buried, the sister reminds her.

He has no right to stop me, the young woman exclaims. She turns to her sister...

Be what seems right to you;
Him will I bury. Death, so met, were honor;
And for that capital crime of piety,
loving and loved, I will lie at his side.
Far longer is there need I satisfy
Those nether powers, than powers on earth; for there
Forever must I lie...

The young woman is the Greek princess Antigone, daughter of Oedipus and sister of the dead Polynices who has been killed in an expedition to win the throne of Thebes. Creon, the King of Thebes, has decreed that Polynices' body should remain unburied, but Antigone will not allow that to happen even though she knows that violation of Creon's decree will mean death.

Here, then, is the story line for one of the great Greek tragedies by Sophocles. *Antigone* explores the basic question of whether one's duty is first to the gods or to the state. When the laws are in conflict, which should prevail?

For the ancient Greeks, leaving a body unburied was the most heinous of all events because it meant the soul would be sentenced to grievous torment. Proper burial was not only the obligation of the family but an act of piety demanded by the gods, and failure to appease the gods brought untold misery and suffering. Thus Antigone's dilemma... does she obey King Creon's law or does she follow her conscience and the will of the gods?

It's a classic case of self-sacrifice. Antigone, knowing the consequences of her actions, pursues her goal because it represents a purpose higher than the vengeance exacted by Creon on Polynices' body. Self-sacrifice is just this: giving oneself up because something or someone is more important. A cause, an ideal, even an act of self-regeneration is what motivates self-sacrifice. Think of it as a balancing... which of two or three alternatives is more important? Do they balance one another? If one weighs more, do we bring them back in balance again by self-sacrifice?

Antigone, even though she is engaged to Creon's son, Haemon, is sentenced to die, and she is placed in a cave which is then walled up. But the prophet, Tiresias, warns Creon that the gods are not happy with the way he has handled things. Bury Polynices, he suggests, release Antigone, or Haemon will die.

Creon realizes that Tiresias's prophesies have never proven

false. He rushes to have Polynices buried and to release Antigone. At the mouth of the cave he hears Haemon, inside, crying out with grief. When he enters he finds Antigone dead, hung by a rope from her own garment, and Haemon rushes at his father, spits at him and then falls on his own sword. He, too, is dead in seconds.

When Creon's wife hears about her son, she kills herself. Creon, in deep anguish, then admits he has been wrong. He gives up his throne and has himself exiled from the city.

The self-sacrifice, here, of course, is Antigone's, and in the dilemma over whether to obey the laws of man or the laws of the gods we have an often-used plot. Lloyd Douglas uses it, for example, in *The Robe*, and Henryk Sienkiewicz uses it in *Quo Vadis*, both of which highlight the conflict between the birth of Christianity and the opposition of the Romans. Self-sacrifice for a higher ideal — in this case a place in the Christian orbit — makes hommage to Roman law a lesser responsibility. One sacrifices oneself for this greater ideal even though it may mean death.

We can take any moral imperative and apply the self-sacrifice formula. It doesn't need to be religion-based, just something that demands a right — or righteous — course of action. We sacrifice ourselves because we have a conscience.

And speaking of conscience, one of the most remarkable examples in literature is found in Leo Tolstoy's *Resurrection*, the story of a Russian prince, landed gentry in Czarist Russia, who sacrifices almost all he has for a prostitute. The story begins when Prince Nekhludoff seduces Katusha who is just sixteen years old and the ward of Nekhludoff's aunt. She becomes pregnant and has the baby, but it dies soon after birth. Nekhludoff, meanwhile, pursues a military career, ignorant of what is happening.

In fact it is ten years later that Nekhludoff, now wealthy and a playboy, sees Katusha again, and then only by chance. He sits

making amends, certainly. (In fact, this one will appear frequently in stories of self-sacrifice.) There's loss of material well-being, rescue, and honor and dishonor. A bagful of spicers for a vivid story of self-sacrifice.

A woman's a woman and a man's a man, and well . . . through the ages one or the other has sacrificed a lot for love. This is especially true when the love isn't returned. Nekhludoff's sacrifice for Katusha is essentially for love, and his ultimate hope is to help her, even though in the end they go their separate ways.

Literature is full of such sacrifices for love, and one of the more notorious is that depicted in Somerset Maugham's *Of Human Bondage*, where the woman — Mildred — is not such a likable character as is Katusha. Mildred, in fact, spends years duping a young medical student, Phillip Carey, into giving her money, supporting her, rescuing her and slavishly waiting on her — all because he loves her. Carey, with his club foot (one aspect of the bondage in the title), is enthralled with the worldly wise, older woman, and for years he thinks she returns his feelings. Though, of course, it isn't so; she goes out with other men, goes off with them too and uses Phillip only when she has nowhere to turn. In fact, Carey's love for Mildred is the other aspect of the bondage in the book's title.

How does she view the way Phillip feels? After she has another man's child and Phillip is back in her life because she needs money and a place to live, she considers that now she should settle down with him . . . "She had no doubt of her power over him . . . He had so often quarrelled with her and sworn he would never see her again, and then in a little while he had come on his knees begging to be forgiven. It gave her a thrill to think how he had cringed before her. He would have been glad to lie down on the ground for her to walk on him. She had seen him cry. She knew exactly how to treat him, pay no attention to him, just pretend you didn't notice his tempers, leave him severely alone, and in a little while he was sure to grovel."

What Phillip sacrifices for Mildred isn't his fortune or his power. What he gives up is his honor, his sense of self-respect. He becomes her slave, her rag doll she can kick around whenever she feels like it. For Phillip the cause is sufficient — his love for her. He would do anything for that. And, of course, he does.

Did Maugham steal Tolstoy's plot? Only in the very general sense that a man will give up things he might hold dear for the love of a woman. Maugham doesn't get into the biblical yardstick of spiritual atonement the way Tolstoy does. For Maugham, Phillip Carey's actions are sufficiently explained by his love for Mildred and his hope of having her love him back. Fulfillment — spiritual, physical or any other kind — would follow naturally.

There are infinite variations on the man-woman theme with self-sacrifice. Perhaps the woman becomes the man's slave, or they jointly sacrifice for the love of a third person — a child or a parent — or they sacrifice themselves for each other or they sacrifice themselves not out of love but out of vengeance on one another.

Men and women don't have to be in love in order to sacrifice for one another. There are other motivations just as strong. Take Jan de Hartog's 1960 novel *The Inspector* which concerns the actions of Peter Jongman, a member of the criminal investigation department in the Amsterdam police department. The story is set in 1946 and Jongman is on the trail of a white-slave trader who takes young girls to South America and places them in brothels against their wishes. Jongman is a bit unsettled. In his youth he had wanted to be a sailor but instead had opted for the security of a police career. Then, during the war, he stayed in his comfortable job while the Nazis held the country. He was able to free a few anti-Nazi criminals, but compared to the work of the underground his contribution wasn't much.

Now, as he follows the white-slave trader to London and confronts him, his eyes lock with a thin-faced girl, Anna Held, whom the slave trader is about to ship out. Jongman demands the girl be set free, and the white slave trader shrugs and answers, "What do any of them matter? They are Jewish bitches that slipped through the net! This one is from a medical research camp. She is no good to anybody. She has even been sterilized!"

In the ensuing days Jongman finds that Anna wants to go to Israel, and he thinks of how little he really did during the war. If he were to help her get to Israel, wouldn't that make up for some of his doubts?

The journey, then, to Israel becomes his regeneration. He must undertake it in defiance of most of the governments in the world who back the British in closing off all emigration to Israel. He also runs the risk of losing his wife and family because, of course, he will make the trip alone with Anna. So he is faced with the ultimate form of self-sacrifice: he stands to lose his job, his wife and family and his life.

Is it done for the love of Anna? Yes and no. He comes to love her, but he has no urge for sexual relations. It is a platonic love, a joy simply in giving to another human being without expecting anything in return. He comes to see that what he is doing is necessary to save his soul, and that if he survives, he will not be the same smugly assured, narrowly based person he was. For him there is no doubt — the sacrifices are worth it.

Self-sacrifice is really nothing more than giving up something we have or something we hold in esteem in order to gain something else we consider more important. Another person stands to benefit in all this, and so we sacrifice ourselves or part of ourselves for that other person. Antigone does it for the soul of her dead brother, Polynices; Prince Nekhludoff does it for Katusha, Phillip Carey does it for Mildred; Peter Jongman does it for Anna Held. The relationships which offer the opportunity for self sacrifice are as varied as the human mind can extend because what we're limited by isn't who can or can't sacrifice for whom. Anyone can play this game, anyone can be a self-sacrificer. The only limitation is whether one really sacrifices or not. The key is just what is being given up, why, and what is expected in return. Self-sacrifice demands a substantial commitment. Without it there really wouldn't be much of a story.

Suppose, for example, a man finds his wife is very ill, and he is faced with a dilemma: should he give up his girlfriend in order to devote all available time to his wife in her last months, trying to make those last few months as comfortable as possible? If he does, and in the course of caring for his wife he finds that he has really been in love with her all this time, do we have any self-sacrifice in his breaking off with his girlfriend? Perhaps, in the beginning, but even so, how much of a sacrifice is he really making? What is the cause or ideal he is seeking in such sacrifice? To make his wife's final time comfortable? As a humanitarian gesture it is certainly admirable, but is it strong enough to support something we think of as self-sacrifice? Especially when he is seeing the girlfriend right up to the moment he makes the decision?

Now, what if... his wife wants to go on a final journey, somewhere far away, and it is dangerous and costly and questionable that either or both will return safely. To give up his girlfriend in these circumstances is much more story-provoking. Here he gives up much more, including the possibility of remaining alive. *That* is self-sacrifice.

Giving up one's life is the ultimate sacrifice. Stories of a hero striding fearlessly into almost certain death so that something or someone else can live have come down to us from the Greeks (the legend of Theseus and the Minotaur, for example). They embody the idea that even in death there will be some kind of purification and regeneration. The person who sacrifices will live in the minds of those he saved, and his memory will be treated with deference and respect.

A natural place for this type of situation is in stories of intrigue, suspense, revolution, even war. Any circumstances where the concept of death and dying is a normal outgrowth of the action. Stories with political undercurrents are especially appealing...

Take *Days of Wrath*, written by André Malraux in 1936. It's the story of Kassner, a Communist who has been arrested by the Nazis in Germany. Kassner is one of the Nazis' most-wanted people, but they don't know that the man they have is Kassner, and so they don't kill him summarily. Instead they spend nine days torturing him, trying to get him to divulge who Kassner is and where to find him. He is kept for hours in a pitch-black cell, disoriented and terror-filled in a way he never felt when he was facing danger out in the streets. But he doesn't break, though his mind is swirling with jumbled thoughts, and he is close to losing his sanity.

Then he hears a tapping on the wall... "Comrade, comrade, take courage..." That's all, nothing more.

Suddenly from the adjoining cell he hears sounds of the guards beating someone — muffled noises and shouts. Shortly, he's hauled from his cell and sped off into the countryside. He's given two days to leave the country.

His head is filled with questions. But then he hears one of the guards talking. Another man, it seems, has admitted he is Kassner. He has given himself up for a certain death.

And the real Kassner doesn't know who the man is. But this nameless stranger gives his life so Kassner can live and continue his work.

Malraux, quite obviously, is writing a form of revolutionary fiction here. Remember the date — 1936, the zenith of strains between the Nazis and the Communists throughout Europe. Malraux was a Communist himself, ardently subscribing to the revolutionary philosophy, so of course he paints his hero in glittering hues. But that doesn't detract from the fact that this story is motivated by self-sacrifice. A good writer can recognize strong motivations and dramatize them so the story can go forward, even if he or she may not be in agreement with those motivations. The point is that Malraux believed the ideals of revolution were good enough motivators to construct a story of self-sacrifice.

A man dies for his political beliefs. Isn't that a strong enough motivator? Especially when he allows someone else to live and perpetuate those beliefs?

12

Survival

Some plot motivators are simply better than others at generating a story line, and stories about survival are clearly among the best. Why? Because a survival story contains the major elements for any tale — natural tension over whether survival will in fact take place, a backdrop that constantly menaces the characters, and built-in conflicts. There can be conflict over the *way* to survive, *who* will survive, and even *when* to survive.

For example, in the classic survival story we have someone in an alien environment, remote from other people (or in company with others in the same position) and dependent upon his or her skills. How the characters cope and whether or not they succeed are the keys to the story. We can use what if... over and over: what if... the setting is the jungle and the characters are all city-oriented? What if... the characters are arch rivals and only one holds the key to survival? What if... one of the characters falls in love with another character and affects both their wills to survive? What if... survival depends on the skills of one person and he/she refuses to help? What if... coping with survival brings out hidden talents and hidden flaws in each of the characters? What if... one or more of the characters doesn't want to survive? What if... the menace to survival turns out to be something different from what everyone thought? What if... among the survivors is someone who has criminal designs on another? What if... the survivors turn on one another out of desperation and frustration?

What's clear is that survival is an excellent springboard. And we can make some pretty accurate generalities with respect to using survival as a plot motivator. For example, survival will usually follow some catastrophe, some event that has cast the survivors to the place where we find them. So, it would be possible to treat the plot motivator, catastrophe, in the same way as we treat survival, except that the emphasis would be placed on surviving. Paul Gallico does this with his 1969 book, *The Poseidon Adventure*. It is the story of a luxury cruise-ship caught by an underwater earthquake (the catastrophe). The ship capsizes but somehow stays afloat, and a small party of passengers must make their way from the overturned main deck up through the bowels of the ship to the tip of the floating hull. How they do it is the story of survival, and the leader is an athlete turned minister who uses his mountaineering skills to lead the people to safety. Even as the characters survive, however, the elements of the catastrophe are all around and so they must be treated. There's the menace of drowning or some other death while crawling through the ship's innards, the fact that there was no way to prepare for the disaster, and the stark depiction of ruin and shambles all around.

Yet where catastrophe presupposes death and destruction, survival emphasizes life and rescue. Survival comes *after* catastrophe and should carry with it a greater degree of hope.

In addition, catastrophe stories tend to be monumental, taking in large numbers of people and places. But survival stories can be limited to one person in one place. The basic question continues to surface: will he/she survive or not? The ordeal, in other words, can be reduced to a single individual's struggle.

In survival stories, too, the story spicer, rescue, is almost always in the picture. Will the survivor/survivors be rescued or not? Perhaps one can survive and not be rescued, in the sense that one can rescue oneself, but usually the hope for outside rescue permeates these stories.

No more vivid portrait of the hope for rescue and the urge to survive can be found in all of literature than that of Daniel Defoe's legendary character, Robinson Crusoe. Of all survival stories, this one comes to mind first. Robinson, a young Englishman with a taste for adventure, is aboard a ship which breaks up on reefs off the coast of South America in the latter part of the seventeenth century. Only he survives, of all the crew and passengers, and he washes ashore on an uninhabited island. He is able to retrieve food, ammunition, water, wine, clothing, tools, sailcloth and lumber from the stricken ship, and thus begins his thirty-five year sojourn on the island. Yet Robinson never loses hope that he will be rescued, even though he sets about building himself a permanent shelter and furniture. He learns to trap and plant, and creates for himself a self-perpetuating little world.

His first sight of other humans occurs after 24 years, and they are cannibals who devour human flesh before his eyes. But because he still has guns, he is able to rescue a prisoner of theirs who becomes Friday, his long-time and trusted servant. Now, after a quarter century of seeing no one, he has companionship, but of course Friday can speak no English. So Robinson begins to teach him. Another ten years pass, and then an English ship appears off the island. Robinson and Friday rush down to greet a ship's party as they come ashore. The party, however, is just the Captain and two crew members, victims of a mutiny.

Robinson and the Captain, along with Friday and the two

seamen, retake the vessel, and finally Robinson Crusoe returns to his native England, after 35 years. The major thrust of the story, of course, is not the rescue but the manner in which Robinson survives. He washes ashore with absolutely nothing — only what he is able to save from the ship. He is not skilled in outdoor survival, nor in planting, carpentry or hunting. Yet he is able to pull it off because of sheer determination, a little luck and an intelligence that refuses to panic but carefully and methodically creates a way of life. This is a perfect story of survival, combining the elements alluded to above: he is in an alien environment, remote from others and dependent solely upon his own skills. There is as much fascination in how he survives as in whether he survives. And that is really a key to survival stories: readers like to watch the step-by-step process of survival, they can easily identify with the protagonist as he/she struggles and copes, and they can not with approval as he/she takes each hesitant step.

The remote-island setting is perhaps the most familiar device for stories of survival because it provides a very appropriate format for man-against-nature plots. The conflicts and the tensions are apparent from the beginning; the writer doesn't have to go about constructing them, as is the case with stories of rivalry or betrayal or even persecution. Man-against-nature is the classic survival story, and it can be even more exciting if man-against-man is added to the mix. Then there is a double conflict and the undoubted appearance of other plot motivators.

Man versus man... try *Lord of the Flies*, William Golding's fine book written in 1955. Here we have the remote island setting. A group of young English boys, the oldest of which is twelve, are the victims of a plane crash on a tropic island after the outbreak of world-wide nuclear war. They are alone, without parents or other adults, and they must learn to cope. The story is essentially that — coping, surviving in an alien environment and without adult assistance. But the man-versus-nature theme is quickly subverted to the man-versus-man theme as the boys in just a few weeks begin to fashion themselves a society built along familiar English lines. They call an assembly and elect a leader. They set up rules, give everyone tasks to do. But shortly things begin to deteriorate. In the tropic heat they shed their clothes, and they find pleasure in painting their bodies. They elect two chiefs, Ralph and Jack. Ralph is the methodical one, concerned with preserving the structure of whatever civilization they have, while Jack is the maverick, a rebel who quickly comes to odds with Ralph. "Rules are the only thing we've got!" says Ralph, while Jack responds, "____ to the rules!"

The boys split into two groups, forming rivalries and hatreds. The fat boy in the group, Piggy, becomes the ultimate scapegoat who succeeds in saving the boys at the cost of his life. This story is really an allegory on the human condition and the fact that the civilized behavior we have spent thousands of years developing can actually be dissipated in a matter of weeks. At first the boys think of their situation as high adventure, but it doesn't take long for them to realize they are alone in an alien world, unprepared except for what little they have learned in their short lives. This is when, even as they try to follow the highly civilized example of English society in setting up a governing structure, they begin to succumb to the primitiveness all around them. The adventure turns to nightmare as torture and cruelty replace the early optimism that English manners can serve anywhere, anytime.

Did Golding steal this plot? What if... a group of children are captured and placed aboard a pirate ship sometime in the nineteenth century and exposed to murder, seduction and the grim outlaw life. And what if... the gradual maturing of the children causes them to accept or reject this way of life with equal fervor, even as the pirate ship goes about its deadly business, murdering and pillaging at will? And what if...

rivalries and hatreds occur between and among the children as they seek or reject special favors from the pirates?

A quarter century before *Lord of the Flies*, Richard Hughes wrote *A High Wind in Jamaica*, a tale of children living aboard a pirate vessel based on a true incident. Hughes's story, like Golding's, is a view of the child's world in the midst of chaos and remoteness, *as viewed by the child or children*. In both books the setting is outside the normal bounds of civilization — an uninhabited tropic island or an outlaw pirate ship. Laws and rules and manners are what the individual participants say they are, and yet there is a certain rough civility. Emily, ten years old and precocious, is accosted one night by the drunken pirate-ship captain in *A High Wind in Jamaica*, but she bites his thumb and he moves off. For days she and the Captain avoid one another until Emily is injured when a dropped marlin spike severely damages her thigh. The Captain comes along, sober now, but instead of attacking her he takes her to his cabin where he dresses the wound and allows her to sleep in his bunk.

The rough civility in *Lord of the Flies* is apparent from the time the boys decide to organize along accepted English governing principles, with elected leaders and rules of conduct. That even within these bounds of civility there can be cruelty and viciousness is also apparent. And in this sense there is little distinction from what goes on in *A High Wind in Jamaica*. The point of both books is this: survival in an alien world is a learning process that forces us to examine the very essence of who we are and to cope with what we find. Seen through children's eyes, survival is different and much less fearful because of the essential innocence of childhood. That innocence becomes clouded as children mature, and the fearlessness with which survival was once approached is now replaced with uncertainty and, at times, total fear.

The remote-island setting for books like *Lord of the Flies* and *Robinson Crusoe* or fictional extensions like the floating derelict in *The Poseidon Adventure* or outlaw-pirate society in *A High Wind in Jamaica* are only a few of the possibilities where survival as a plot motivator could take shape. What if we use... an abandoned railroad car... or a remote cave... or a prison cell or prison camp... or a sealed bank vault? Each provides the necessary alien atmosphere for the story to take shape. But these aren't the only settings we can use.

Suppose survivability depends, not on place, but on person? Suppose it isn't *where* we are that's so important but *who* we are that helps to motivate the story? Suppose we take an otherwise ordinary person and place that person in extraordinary circumstances and see what they would do? There's little of the remote-island kind of setting in this approach, though of course such a setting could be used. But the story of survival doesn't have to work within the confines of a narrow physical atmosphere. It, instead, can have elements of the chase and mistaken identity, and the menace can be more human than environmental (in other words the survivor is fighting off other people rather than a stark, forbidding element).

Such a story is what John Buchan wrote in 1915. *The Thirty-Nine Steps* has become the basis for many tales of mystery and suspense in the ensuing years. Graham Greene writes of Buchan that he was "the first to realize the enormous dramatic value of adventure in familiar surroundings happening to unadventurous men." His story is essentially one of survival in the face of a well directed, well financed adversary against the background of the events leading to the First World War.

Richard Hannay, a mining engineer in London, is suddenly confronted by another tennant in his building, Franklin Scudder, who tells a fantastic tale about plans for the assassination of a Greek diplomat who is about to visit London. Scudder is badly frightened because his knowledge of the plot has brought him to the attention of The Black Stone, a secret organization that wants nothing better than to start a war between England and

Germany. The assassination will help in the plan immeasurably. Hannay lets Scudder stay in his flat, but he returns one day to find Scudder with a knife through his heart. Then he notices two men patrolling in front of the building.

He's convinced now that The Black Stone knows who he is and that his own life is in danger. He retrieves a little black book from Scudder's body that he had seen Scudder makes notes in. Then he escapes from his flat in disguise, planning to stay in hiding for a couple of weeks and then divulge what he knows to the authorities.

He goes to Scotland, but he finds that the London papers have reported Scudder's murder and his own description and that he is suspected of committing the murder. He finds a refuge, but one day a plane flies overhead, and he assumes The Black Stone has found him, so he flees again (notice that Hannay has nothing on his mind but surviving, and thus this is a story of survival — an ordinary man in extraordinary circumstances). Another time he is briefly captured by The Black Stone but succeeds in getting away.

He reads Scudder's black book and sees it is in code which he arduously tries to decipher. He succeeds, finally, and finds that Scudder has told him only part of the truth. Yes, there will be the planned assassination of the Greek diplomat, but also there is to be an armed invasion of England, with airfields already laid out and mines to be placed along the shoreline. A French envoy with plans for the placement of the British fleet is to be intercepted so that the exact arrangement of the mines can be made. The operation is to commence at a place where there are thirty-nine steps and a high tide at 10:47 P.M. No other information can be uncovered by Hannay.

Then he has a stroke of luck and meets someone with high connections in the British government. All the while, of course, The Black Stone is still after him, and so he must be very careful. But he finally gets to someone in the government and convinces him about the plot.

There is to be a secret government meeting concerning the information Hannay has provided, but Hannay is not invited. However, his sixth sense tells him he should go. Without telling anyone, he appears at the house and sits in the hallway waiting to be called. While he is waiting, one of the officials at the meeting comes out, and Hannay recognizes him as a member of The Black Stone — someone he had seen when he had been briefly held by them. Hannay turns out to be right, and the man, who by now has escaped, is seen as an imposter for the First Lord of the Admiralty. While in the meeting, the imposter has scanned the entire defense structure of England from drawings and figures on the tables.

Hannay, finally, has been rescued, and his ordeal as a survivor is now over. The book goes on showing how Hannay uncovers the secrets of the thirty-nine steps and the time and place in the reference to high tide. The end result is that even though England and Germany declare war on one another in a matter of weeks, the war will not be fought on British soil, which the author points out might have happened if the plot by The Black Stone has succeeded.

Buchan's thriller is the model for so many works which followed, particularly because of the presence of another plot motivator, the chase. The story revolves around Hannay surviving while being chased by The Black Stone and by the authorities. How he survives is important, of course, but more important is why he should survive. It is the theme of good guys versus bad guys, and here, at least the good guys will win. In one sense the alien atmosphere we find in *Lord of the Flies* or *The Poseidon Adventure* or any of the other works set on remote islands is also present here. Isn't Hannay's situation just as alien to a civilized, law-abiding man as forbidding terrain would be to a group of young English boys? Hannay must try and stay alive and deliver some vital information to the proper people, efforts he has not had to make, nor been trained for. So, in this sense, at least, his world is just as alien, just as forbidding.

An up-to-date equivalent of *The Thirty Nine Steps* is James Dickey's *Deliverance* where four men decide to white-water canoe a wilderness river before it will be lost forever to a dam and the demands of civilization. These are not macho types, but soft, paunchy suburbanites with a mild yen for adventure. But their fun turns to terror as they run across some vengeful backwoodsmen, and before it's over one of the adventurers is killed and the others have barely survived. The key to this story, as with Buchan's tale, is the actions of ordinary men suddenly confronted by difficult, unusual circumstances. How do they handle it?

One falls apart, another calls on a reserve of courage and endurance to lead them through while a third remains badly injured. The fourth has been killed. Here again, the chase plays an important part because the men are stalked by the woodsmen who have every intention of killing them. They start out as the hunted, but in the end they become the hunters, and that is how they survive. The chase and survival work hand in hand with these stories.

Actually, what is survival but a state of mind? No matter where we find ourselves we either cope or we don't. Stories of survival are essentially this. And when we write them, we are limited only by the settings our imagination can cook up.

13

Rivalry

Lydia, the heroine, is young, vivacious and addicted to reading sentimental romantic fiction...

Jack, the hero, is handsome, rich and determined to win Lydia...

Anthony, Jack's father, wants him to marry someone Anthony will choose...

Lydia's aunt favors Bob, Lydia's *other* suitor, who is also rich and aspires to become a man about town...

Jack has been seeing Lydia under an assumed name because he realizes that if she knew him under his real name, she would have nothing to do with him. For her the true pursuit of romance is what she has found in the melodramatic, sentimental love stories she reads incessantly. The person she will fall in love with must be dashing, certainly, but also penniless. And Jack, if she knew the truth, is far from penniless!

So is Bob, Lydia's *other* suitor, but then he has Lydia's aunt pushing his availability. To the aunt, Jack appears just as Lydia sees him — poor, struggling, yet handsome and debonair. Bob, the *other* suitor, however, has all the characteristics one would want in a husband — reliability, saneness, wealth, loyalty, ambition — and family approval.

Anthony, Jack's father, however, becomes determined that his son should marry the *right* person, and he astounds Jack by proposing it be Lydia. But Lydia doesn't know Jack under his real name, and Anthony doesn't know Jack is already taken with Lydia, but in his disguised capacity. The father, who doesn't know Jack and Lydia already know one another, decides his son should meet Lydia, which complicates things even more because Lydia only knows Jack in a disguise.

What to do? In his disguise Jack attempts to convince Lydia that because her aunt doesn't like him, he must pretend to be someone else... and he reassumes his natural identity. But Lydia, her dreams of love with a poor, though good man no longer a reality, will have nothing to do with him.

In the meantime, Bob, the *other* suitor, has discovered he has a rival. So he challenges Jack to a duel... only he has never seen Jack and so he assumes his rival is someone else, only it is actually Jack-in-disguise because that is the only way Bob has heard about him. He also hears that Jack is friendly with the character Jack has assumed — himself in disguise. So he gives the challenge to Jack to transmit to the person whose identity Jack has assumed.

Before the duel can be fought, Lydia rushes to the field of honor, now taken with the fact that Jack, even though he may be rich, would fight a duel for her. A new, romantic scene blossoms before her... she realizes that Jack and the person she wanted to be her hero are the same individual! Ah, that a man, any man, would fight a duel on her behalf!

Bob, the *other* suitor breathes a sigh of relief because now he is forced to fight a duel no longer... and he can reassume his man-about-town role.

"It almost seems," wrote Samuel Butler in the nineteenth century, "as though the nearer people stand to one another in respect of either money or genius, the more jealous they become of one another..."

A good point, because in the dramatic situation above the rivals for Lydia, the heroine, are both rich and both determined, and jealousy is inherent in the scope of the rivalry. Jealousy and rivalry don't always go together easily because jealousy will sometimes spring from covetousness that someone has something or someone the other wants. Rivalry, of course, implies that neither has the prize as yet. However, jealousy and rivalry come together when they are both founded on the idea that one is *aware* of a competitor for something or someone and that there can be only one winner.

In fact, in the dramatic situation above, we are talking about the essence of rivalry — it is Richard Brinsley Sheridan's classic satire on affectation and eighteenth-century English upper-class manners, *The Rivals*. The plot is basic — two men in love with the same woman — but, of course, it's only the beginning. By injecting the plot motivator, rivalry, into the story, Sheridan has brought along a variety of elements: jealousy, competition, conflict, success. But most important he has also used the story spicer, mistaken identity. The entire story is moved along because everyone has a mistaken notion about everyone else. By carrying it to outlandish extremes, Sheridan has used a basic humor-technique — exaggeration. *The Rivals* is comedy even though it may be a bit stiff for our taste today. Sheridan satirizes the superficiality and the empty-headedness of the upper-class English by showing them as objects of derision. He exaggerates their foibles, and in so doing he makes us laugh.

Did Sheridan steal this plot? Take a look at the Shakespearean comedy, *Two Gentlemen From Verona*. Two good friends, Valentine and Proteus, go their separate ways, Valentine to Milan to pursue his fortune at the palace of the Duke. Proteus stays in Verona happily content with his love for Julia. In Milan, Valentine meets Sylvia, the Duke's daughter, and falls in love. The Duke, however, wants Sylvia to marry Thurio, a wealthy though foolish landowner. Then Proteus shows up in Milan, sent there by his father who wants him to become more worldly. Valentine introduces him to Sylvia and confides that he intends to put a rope ladder up to Sylvia's room and steal her from under her father's nose. Proteus, however, can't bear the thought of Valentine going off with Sylvia because he, Proteus, has also fallen for her in spite of his earlier vows of love for Julia. So Proteus goes to the Duke and tells him of Valentine's plan. The Duke then banishes Valentine from Milan.

Julia, however, now shows up in Milan disguised as a page and thinking Proteus still loves her. She comes to Sylvia's house and stands in the shadows while Proteus sings love songs to Sylvia. But Sylvia will have none of it, saying she still loves Valentine and that Proteus should be ashamed of the way he is treating Julia.

Proteus doesn't give up so easily and decides to send messages to Sylvia via the nearest page — who happens to be Julia in disguise. In the end Proteus sees that Sylvia truly loves Valentine and that Julia, her disguise now lifted, is the one for him. Valentine returns from exile, gains the Duke's favor and is betrothed to Sylvia.

There are differences with *The Rivals*, of course. But Shakespeare uses the identical story spicer, mistaken identity, and he has one of the suitors in disfavor with the young woman's authority figure. In *The Rivals* the two young men almost fight a duel. In *Two Gentlemen From Verona* Proteus and Valentine end up wrestling and fighting for Sylvia. Shakespeare's use of deception as a story spicer comes off in a bit more subtle fashion than in Sheridan's work — Proteus betraying Valentine to the Duke — but in both stories deception is a definite factor in the way the plot moves. In Thurio, Shakespeare has a character very similar to the *other* suitor in *The Rivals*: wealthy, a bit priggish with social class aspirations.

So... did Sheridan steal Shakespeare's plot? Maybe steal is too strong a word. After all, we really don't know if Sheridan had ever read Shakespeare, though it's fairly common knowledge that Shakespeare's plays and poems were well recognized and read by the last third of the eighteenth century.

Suppose we say that two fine dramatists happened to fashion similar stories, even though they lived two centuries apart. As we've said, what's the crime in a bit of plot larceny?

More than a century after Sheridan, Edmond Rostand uses rivalry as a plot motivator in his *Cyrano de Bergerac*. The story is well known: Cyrano, a poet, loves Roxanne, but he composes love poems for his friend, Christian, letting Roxanne think Christian is the poet. Note the similarity with Shakespeare and Sheridan: Cyrano and Christian as rivals... and as the objects of mistaken identity.

Humor is here, too. Cyrano shows off his oversized proboscis: "A great nose indicates a great man — genial, courteous, intellectual, virile, courageous..."

But more importantly, the plot is a love story with rivalry the motivating factor. The fact that Christian is oblivious to having a rival only heightens the tension and allows us to identify more with Cyrano. Yet love is the object of the rivalry, and as with *The Rivals* it is the basis of the story.

The general concept of rivalry can be traced back to the early Greek legends. On a broad scale it is found in the continuing rivalry between the city-states, Athens and Sparta. On a more personal level, we need look no further than the conflict between Ajax and Odysseus for the armor of Achilles. During the ten years of the Trojan War Achilles was considered the most fearsome of the Greek warriors. In single combat he destroyed the Trojan hero, Hector, and then paraded his body, lashed to a chariot, around the walls of Troy. But later, Paris, son of the Trojan King, Priam, was able to kill Achilles by shooting a poisoned arrow into his heel, the one place he could not protect. Now it was time for a new Greek champion to emerge and both Ajax, considered second only to Achilles in strength and courage, and Odysseus, claimed that honor. They finally put their cases to Agamemnon, the Greek king. Agamemnon chose Odysseus for the armor, and Ajax went absolutely raving mad, ultimately killing himself.

But for sheer plot magnitude on the theme of rivalry, there is little that can surpass Sir Walter Scott's 1819 epic, *Ivanhoe*. A veritable cornucopia of rivalries are present here, involving love and politics and manliness and property and even religion. It is the time when knighthood is the reigning norm, when Prince John is Regent in England, ruling in place of his brother, Richard the Lion-Hearted who has gone to fight for Christendom in the Crusades. Richard is thought to have been imprisoned somewhere in Austria and Prince John is taking steps to solidify his own rule. The plot in *Ivanhoe* fairly bristles with rivalries, though the most significant are those between Wilfred of Ivanhoe and his enemies. First, there is the Knight Templar, Brian de Bois-Guilbert, an arrogant, pugnacious character whom Ivanhoe meets on horseback in the tournament lists. Ivanhoe enters the tournament disguised, and it's only after he has unhorsed Brian de Bois-Guilbert and has distinguished himself in armed combat that he reveals himself.

Then there's Reginald Front-de-Boeuf who acquires the ancestral castle of Ivanhoe from Prince John after it is seized when Wilfred follows Richard to the Crusades. Reginald continues to maintain his claims, and at one point has an injured, captured Wilfred locked away in his castle... only he doesn't realize it's Wilfred.

Then there's Maurice de Bracy, captain of Prince John's Free Lances, who has fallen for Rowena, ward of the Saxon, Cedric of Rotherwood. Here we see a familiar rivalry because it is Rowena that Wilfred loves too, and in fact it is because of that love that Cedric, Wilfred's father, has banished him and caused him to follow Richard to the Crusades.

When Wilfred (severely injured) and Rowena and Cedric are captured by Reginald and Maurice de Bracy and Brian de Bois-Guilbert and taken to Reginald's castle, de Bracy comes to Rowena's apartment and makes his feelings known. And in the process outlines some of what Wilfred faces...

"Thou art proud, Rowena, and all the fitter therefore to be my wife. Know that my rival, Wilfred of Ivanhoe, is in this castle. It only remains for me to betray the fact to Front-de-Boeuf who would make short work of one whose manor he claims as his own. Richard gave Ivanhoe to Wilfred; John has given it to Front-de-Boeuf. There would be no rivalry for its possession if I were to say one word to the lord of this castle...."

Then there is the Christian-Jewish conflict, for this is a time of strong religious passion. Prominent throughout the book are Issac of York and his daughter, Rebecca. Periodic assaults on Issac and Rebecca by various Normans, including Prince John and Reginald Front-de-Boeuf, mirror narrow religious attitudes and establish the intolerance of the high-riding Normans. But in the end there is a resolution of sorts because Brian de Bois-Guilbert has fallen for Rebecca and offers to renounce his knighthood and a place in Europe for a home and a life with Rebecca in Palestine. This plan is doomed, because Rebecca is to be burned at the stake as a sorceress, and when she demands to be judged by trial by combat, Brian de Bois-Guilbert is named by the Templar Order against her. Wilfred comes to Rebecca's aid, and he and Brian finally meet in combat... only Brian falls over dead before a strong blow can be delivered.

Story spicers abound in *Ivanhoe*. There's deception (as when

Wilfred appears in the tournament in disguise), rescue (as when Wilfred comes to Rebecca's aid in the final battle with Brian de Bois-Guilbert), honor and dishonor (as in the code of chivalry that all characters try to follow), criminal action (as in the capture and imprisonment of Wilfred, Issac, Rowena, Rebecca, Cedric by Reginald, Brian and Maurice de Bracy), conspiracy (as in Prince John's continual efforts to solidify his throne against Richard and do away with the influence of any of Richard's supporters), authority (as in the struggle, mainly political, over who will continue to rule England — Prince John or Richard).

Do we want to steal a plot? There's enough in *Ivanhoe* for all of us to use and still leave a field of possibilities for those coming along afterwards. Rivalry as a plot motivator can find its way into almost any type of situation. In politics, love, religion, physical prowess, the military — any case where two or more people or groups are vying to win something or someone.

Or how about the world of business? Let's deal with a contemporary situation. "A minute or two before or after two-thirty on the afternoon of the twenty-second of June, Avery Bullard suffered what was later diagnosed as a cerebral hemorrhage. After fifty-six years, somewhere deep within the convoluted recesses of his brain, a tiny artery finally yielded to the insistent pounding of his hard-driven bloodstream. In that instant of infinitessimal failure the form and pattern of a world within a world was changed. An industrial empire was suddenly without an emperor..."

So begins *Executive Suite*, a 1952 novel by Cameron Hawley that was also made into a movie. It is the story of what happens to the Tredway Corporation, a large, dynamic multinational business in the twenty-four hours following the sudden death of the man who had taken it from a small, family-owned business almost in bankruptcy and molded it into a major corporation. The story line is rivalry in its raw, pure form with the overriding question pumping through the pages — who will be the next Chief Executive Officer of the Tredway Corporation?

Hawley introduces several contenders, each of them a vice-president of one area of the business, and then he portrays them scheming and plotting against one another to take over the top spot. One tries to manipulate stock holdings, others attempt to influence large shareholders to support them. At times the contenders grow obsequious or demanding as they try to thrust themselves forward. For Hawley, the author, the world of business is not a sharply drawn battlefield of good guys and bad guys, but a place where there are simply better people and worse people, where a businessman's ambition is not so much to be skewered as to be defined and directed. In the various power plays that the characters let loose, one school of thought feels that the financial people ought to be in charge of the business, that there should be emphasis on "safety" and conservation of capital; others feel that there really should be no frontier to business expansion, that a business that doesn't grow is in the throes of dying. In the end, Avery Bullard's successor is someone cut from Bullard's mold, dynamic, forward looking yet balanced. The rivalries have determined who that successor will be.

Stories with a business background are a natural for a plot motivator such as rivalry. The essence of business is competition, and the essence of rivalry is... competition! One feeds the other in a most positive manner, and while the ultimate objective may be money or power or prestige or simply to win for the sake of winning, it is the sense of competition that breeds the rivalry and makes it formidable.

Can we steal the plot of *Executive Suite*? Some say Arthur Hailey modeled his *The Moneychangers* in 1975 after it. The well-loved president of a major bank in the midwestern United States is dying, and as soon as that fact emerges, there is a power struggle for the top spot. Two vice-presidents are involved (not five as in *Executive Suite*) but their differing ideas about where the bank's business should be directed create the rivalry and the competition. One feels that the bank should be a community resource, that it should help the poor and the disadvantaged to upgrade their lives; the other is interested only in the bottom line, the larger the better. In the rivalry between these two concepts we see the same kind of conflict that was apparent in *Executive Suite*, only now it's a quarter-century later. In *The Moneychangers*, an international financial manipulator is pushing the bank for a huge, dangerous loan, and the question is just how far will the bank go in its thirst for profit. Hailey's book, of course, contains various elements not present in *Executive Suite*: there is bank theft, for example, a counterfeit-credit conspiracy and close-at-hand racial problems. Hailey's characters tend to be more good guy-bad guy extremes than do Hawley's, but essentially in both books we have the same story line: a large business leader fades away, and a power struggle for succession occurs. The rivalry is intense and clearly defined between those preferring short-term return and those favoring a longer-term commitment to more human values. Along the way in both books there are story spicers, of course (in *Executive Suite* the question of material wellbeing is important because it keys the issue of safety versus expansion; in *The Moneychangers* criminal action plays a part as does honor and dishonor in the banks' ultimate relations with the local community). But it is rivalry that motivates each plot, and it is rivalry that draws each story line.

Way down, then, at the center of it all, there is that spark of competition that started it off. Because, in the final analysis, we are only rivals when we decide to compete. Rivalry *is* competition.

14

Discovery (Quest)

What if... there's a terrible war, and in its aftermath a young man, a veteran of that war and now displaced, decides to leave his scourged land and find a place for himself elsewhere. He is driven by some inner sense of destiny so that he cannot stay at any one location for very long. Each time he begins to think of settling down, the turmoil within him boils over and he must wander again, never certain where he is headed but absolute in his belief that somewhere, some place will claim him finally.

It is in his quest to fulfill his destiny that this young man wanders, and his life is dotted with adventure and danger and episodes of near-death. A wealthy and influential woman falls in love with him and then kills herself when that love is not returned... a shipwreck nearly kills him and leaves him stranded on the shores of Africa... a local hero resents him so much

that a bitter fued develops and leads them into physical combat . . . a mystical flight of fancy reveals just what his destiny will
be and how he will attain it . . . an assailant wounds him not
once, but twice, as the ultimate battle is fought.

This is the story of the *Aeneid*, the famous epic poem of
Publius Vergilius Maro (Vergil) written in the first century B.C.
It is the tale of the founding of Rome by the Greeks. For Aeneas
there is no going home again, and Vergil paints him as a
wandering hero carrying his destiny while he searches for the
place he will finally settle. It is the story of discovery, the founding of Rome and the beginnings of a civilization, the place
which would become the heartstone of the ancient world.

In some ways Vergil follows the lead of Homer in fashioning
the plot for the *Aeneid*. There are Aeneas's wanderings — quite
similar to those of Odysseus in *The Odyssey* with the usual
assortment of outsized characters and gulp-filled dangers, and
there are the battles which are fought to establish a civilization
on the shores of the Tiber River — quite similar to the battles
and the conflicts in *The Iliad*. Aeneas differs from Odysseus and
some of the others, however, in that his sole motivation for carrying out his destiny is not riches or fame or power but simply
the knowledge that the responsibility has fallen to him to found
a new nation. That, in itself, is sufficient compensation.

When we look at discovery as a plot motivator we must see it,
not as a formula for a chase or a search (though undoubtedly
that could be part of the mix) but as a means of gaining
something or someone through metaphysical considerations. In
other words, it isn't enough to seek physical or tangible rewards;
there must be some extra-physical meaning or compensation.
For example, the quest of Aeneas is not only for a final home
place but for a place where he can found a whole new civilization. His destiny is much broader than merely finding a safe
haven for himself and his men. His is the destiny of the prophet.

There is a sort of other-worldly quality to this plot motivator because stories of discovery often are grounded on elements of self-perception. Whatever we quest for, we have to come to terms with ourselves or the journey hardly seems worth the effort. If Aeneas had decided that the journey and his destiny were simply too long and too difficult to achieve, or that he was content at one of the intermediate stops along his way, or that he really wanted power or riches or the continuing love of one of the beautiful women he encountered, the story would have ended. It would have become an adventure yarn in ancient dress, a story not of epic proportions but simply of minor historical value. By retaining the metaphysical trappings, the *Aeneid* raises the element of discovery to another level and gives it substance and influence.

People wander in stories of discovery. They travel, they search, they seek. There is always a purpose in the wandering, though it might not seem so on superficial investigation. But as with *The Aeneid*, a vague though inner-directed sense of destiny keeps Aeneas going, and his wanderings — to Carthage, Sicily and up the Italian coast — are actually quite purposeful. When he and his men come to the site of the seven hills which would become Rome, they know from a prior prophecy that this is where they will settle.

If wanderings are the name of the game with this plot motivator, then certainly the travels of *Don Quixote de la Mancha* meet the test. In many ways this seventeenth century novel by Miguel Cervantes is the standard by which all other quest novels are judged. "For my absolute faith in the details of their histories," Quixote says, "and my knowledge of their deeds and their characters enable me by sound philosophy to deduce their features, their complexions and their statures." He is speaking of knight-errantry, that cultural and philosophical spur to action, that consumed adventurers and dreamers in the Age of Chivalry. Quixote had read so many chivalric romances that his real world and his fantasy world had melded into a montage of damsels in distress, knightly tournaments, quests, weird and beguiling enchantments. He is so taken with the practice of knight-errantry that he decides to follow its customs and seek out the challenges that the world could present him. He would rescue damsels, he would slay monsters, he would prove his worth in tournaments, he would fight evil and dishonor wherever he could find them. He would revive the long-discontinued practice of knight-errantry. In short, his quest is to deal with a world as it had been centuries before, and to prove his valor as a man under these circumstances.

Of course he is mad, but that doesn't really detract from the book. Cervantes had the avowed purpose of ridiculing the practices of chivalry, and so he established his character in the midst of the most unromantic poses he can find. Quixote is old and poor, his horse, Rosinante, is a mangy old nag, his squire, Sancho Panza, is nothing but an illiterate peasant, his suit of armor belonged to his great grandfather, his mistress, Dulcinea, the one to whom he would dedicate his deeds of valor, is a kitchen-maid who happens to have skill in salting pork.

From all this Quixote sallies forth... and in his first adventure he meets up with some traveling merchants not far from his village. They laugh at him, and then they knock him around when he challenges them to meet him in combat.

Back home he has his cuts and bruises attended to, and his friends, the village priest and the local barber, decide to stop the madness before it goes too far. They burn all his books about chivalry and romance and the code of knight-errantry.

But Quixote is undaunted. His books have been carried off by a wizard, he believes, and he readies himself for another effort to carry the values of knight-errantry to what he believes is a waiting world.

Late at night he and Sancho Panza sneak out of the village, Quixote on his spavined horse and Sancho on a runty donkey.

On the plains of Montiel they see some windmills, and Quixote thinks they are strange, threatening giants. They must be attended to, he decides, and so he sets his lance and kicks Rosinante's flanks until there is a headlong charge, and one of the vanes picks him right out of the saddle and sends him flying.

Why, the giants turned into windmills, he exclaims to Sancho as he is dusted off. Sorcerers must have done this!

Thus Quixote's series of adventures continues. He encounters a lady in a carriage escorted by men on horseback and, thinking her held prisoner, demands her release. There is a sword fight of sorts which Quixote miraculously wins, sparing the life of his victim if he will return to Dulcinea and become her servant; he intervenes in a love quarrel and is soundly beaten for his pains; he mistakes dust clouds for two medieval armies in combat, only to find instead that the clouds are flocks of sheep, and when he intervenes, the shepherds throw rocks because he has scattered the sheep; one night he comes upon a funeral procession but mistakes it for a parade of monsters and attacks, sending the mourners in all directions. For this Sancho names him the Knight of the Sorry Aspect.

The adventures pile up, but the point is that it is the quest of Quixote to re-establish the code of conduct for the knight-errant that moves the story along. Monsters and threats and ladies in danger and feats of valor are the grist for his mill, and he seeks them out with bravery and conscience. It is not enough to read *Don Quixote de la Mancha* as a satire on the ridiculous extremes to which chivalry pushed its adherents; it must also be read as a morality lesson. Is it right to deride someone who wants to perform decent, humanitarian tasks, even though the way they do so may be a bit silly? Can a person not choose the way he or she will live a high-minded life? Are the habits of the past so dead that they can never be resurrected and applied with equal value?

In the end Quixote answers these questions in the simplest

way. Before he dies he renounces knight-errantry as foolish nonsense, never realizing that even though the acts he performed might have been ridiculous in a modern age, the manner in which he conducted himself was in the very spirit of the great knights-errant. He was the true embodiment of the chivalric gentleman. He had succeeded in his quest.

Story spicers in a story like this — or in *The Aeneid*, for that matter — abound. From deception through conspiracy to honor and dishonor (especially this latter) each of the spicers appears, lending substance to a fine tale. Would *The Aeneid* be so powerful if elements of rescue hadn't been present? Would *Don Quixote de la Mancha* be so finely drawn if searching and mistaken identity weren't present? Clearly, in a story which is motivated by discovery, each of the thirteen story spicers could be used.

For example, if we steal the plot of *The Aeneid* and substitute a buried treasure for the destiny of Aeneas to found Rome, then we could introduce story spicers such as criminal action, material well-being, even suicide and suspicion. Not that these aren't present, but to a much lesser extent than they might if we change the plot around to emphasize the physical rather than the metaphysical aspects of the quest. The point is that the nature of the quest will determine the extent and even the usefulness of the individual story spicers. Some work with one type of quest, others work with another. Dabble, experiment, float them and see which sails best.

A quest is really a search for truth, for some definable product that will enlighten us. In *The Aeneid* and *Don Quixote de la Mancha* the quest is essentially positive, a reaffirmation that goodness and virtue can be attained. But there is another side, where a quest seemingly pursued with right-thinking motives can result in something else. Stories of discovery don't always have happy endings, the quest need not be so uplifting.

This is the way it works out in Joseph Conrad's *Heart of Darkness*, the plot of which became the story line for the 1979 movie, *Apocalypse Now!* In Conrad's tale, Marlowe, a young sailor, is to take command of a river steamer that will navigate the inner reaches of the Congo River in Africa to help bring out ivory that has been cut and is awaiting shipment. The sailor hears tales of the legendary Kurtz who lives among the natives, educating them while at the same time sending back record shipments of ivory. Over and over Marlowe hears of Kurtz's reputation and his skill at gaining the natives' respect and confidence. This runs counter to the feelings of the company district manager on the scene who resents what Kurtz is trying to do. He'll ruin the natives, the district manager feels — he's botching up the ivory business.

The quest here is Kurtz's. Can he discover how to help the natives, enlighten them while at the same time providing the company with record quantities of ivory? At first it all seems to be working, but when Marlowe and the district manager finally arrive on scene in the deep-up-country portion of the Congo River, they come face to face with the real truth. Instead of enlightening the natives, Kurtz has been debased by them. He attends native rituals, has killed a number of times in order to get ivory and even hangs shrunken heads outside his door. Kurtz admits to Marlowe the truth of what he has become, asking only that he be allowed to die among the savages he has come to embody. Instead of educating the natives to become like him, he has become more like them.

And in this ironic fact we have the culmination of Kurtz's quest — the truth he seeks is, in effect, a pattern of evil. His discovery is darkness, not light.

Irony can play an important part in stories of discovery. It's a natural plot technique. We establish the nature of the quest right off, and then we slowly build the action towards some kind of resolution. Either we achieve the quest or we don't, but if we don't — or perhaps even if we do — what we ultimately get may not be what we were looking for in the first place.

Take C.P. Snow's 1935 novel, *The Search*. It's the story of a young scientist, Arthur Miles, who, from the age of ten, wants nothing more than to be a scientist, to discover something that will make him notable within the scientific community. For him science is the complete discipline, and his passion for scientific research, the long, arduous hours collecting and evaluating bits and pieces of information are like a sacred journey with the light of eternal truth as the ultimate objective.

Does he find it? Well... yes and no. He becomes a crystallographer and gradually garners the respect and admiration of his colleagues as his learned thoughts and discoveries begin to make the rounds. At one point he falls in love, but even this must give way to his obsession with science. His quest is for immortality within the scientific community and recognition outside it. As he draws closer and closer, his chosen field is suddenly rocked by new thoughts and discoveries, events which make Miles realize he is now on the outside looking in. No longer is he at the cutting edge of his profession — he is now trying to run to catch up.

And in so doing he reflects on whether it has been all worthwhile. He decides that the obsession he held for science was misplaced. Science is but a pleasurable enterprise, providing momentary ecstasy, but for him such ecstasy seemed to arrive only in his youth. In adulthood the ecstasy gives way to pleasure and drive. His quest for immortality in science now becomes, instead, the vehicle for a career change. Ironically, his discoveries in the science field make it possible for him to get close to what he wants, but the closer he gets the more elusive the prize until he decides the quest isn't what he wants anyway.

So he gives up science altogether and starts a career studying and writing about economics. And he is finally content. His discovery has produced an x-ray of himself.

The quest for personal peace is a common theme in stories about discovery. In some there are rights of passage that must be endured, in others only death will finally provide the relief. Personal peace may come through divorce or bankruptcy or sexual release. A final tribute or a final battle may offer lasting comfort. We seek to discover something about ourselves, and the circumstances of that discovery make for a fine plot.

For example, in Margaret Atwood's 1973 novel, *Surfacing*, we have the story of an unhappy, divorced commercial artist, her lover and two friends travelling to the artist's family cabin in a remote section of Quebec in search of the artist's father who has apparently disappeared. While the search goes on, strains among the four travelers begin to appear, and the artist withdraws into a private world full of childhood memories and events. She finds what she considers to be secret clues to the whereabouts of her father, as well as other symbols and signs she believes were left for her by her parents when she was a small child. Pretty soon communication among the four dries up, and the artist slowly sinks into the equivalent of a breakdown, totally immersed in the events of her past. But in effect what is happening is an act of regeneration. The artist has come to the wild, remote Quebec countryside to remove the pain and the anguish of living in a world which holds nothing but discomfort, abuse and disappointment. As she regresses into her past, her quest for some kind of personal peace becomes possible. It may be a private thicket of problems, but at least it is her own thicket and not the product of someone else. In a metaphysical sense she has purified herself, and in so doing she has found peace.

Even where the quest seems to be based on gaining the most tangible of all rewards, there can be another dimension which provides the true essence of what is sought. For example, we wish to discover buried treasure, and so we begin our search. Quite obviously we're looking for material rewards, so can we really call it a quest? It's just a way to get rich, right?

Not necessarily. If our search for treasure brings into question not whether we'll succeed, but why we are trying in the first place, or that what we seek is really just a symbol for something else, then we've gone beyond the physical and into questions of the very nature of the quest.

Such is the intent of Bruno Traven in his 1935 work, *The Treasure of the Sierra Madre*, set in the mountainous wilds of Mexico. It's the story of three down-and-outers who go into the Sierra Madre mountains searching for a lost gold mine. They find the mine and the gold it holds, but then the trouble starts. Traven treats the gold quest in the political sense, as a statement of the sorry mess the profit-making, capitalistic system causes. The men seek to get rich: they can taste the new life that will open up for them... but in their yearning for material rewards — the very reward the capitalistic system offers — they run afoul of the evils of the system.

The three men team up for the gold search, strangers to one another but united in their obsessive quest for the gold. It fills their waking moments, and they talk of little else as they make their trek into the Sierra Madre. The gold mine they seek was once worked by the Spaniards but has long since been abandoned and is reputed to be under an Indian curse. No matter, they proceed anyway, and they do find the gold.

They mine all they can carry, and with pockets bulging they start back to civilization. At this point one of them begins to question why he should have to share with the others. Why shouldn't he keep it all for himself? Another grows ill in a remote Indian village they pass through and reluctantly trusts his gold to the other two. Later, greed becomes a compulsion, and one of the remaining two forces his companion into a clearing in the forest and shoots him in cold blood.

Now he has the gold, and the rich life beckons...

But as he is trudging along, he is suddenly confronted by Mexican bandits. They surround him, and with little concern for the gold dust he is carrying eye his other possessions.

Then — swipe! One of the Mexicans unsheathes a machete and severs the prospector's head from his body... and the gold dust is scattered across the countryside.

An unique plot? It has several story spicers such as honor and dishonor, searching, suspicion, criminal action, material well-being, but these only add substance. The plot is motivated by the quest for gold which turns out to be the basis of evil.

But then, this plot really isn't new. If we go all the way back to the fourteenth century, we see the same story elements in one of Geoffrey Chaucer's *Canterbury Tales*. Specifically, it's *The Pardonner's Tale*, about three men who follow a hedonistic way of life — drinking, gambling, dancing, overeating and wenching. One morning, as they are drinking in their favorite tavern, they hear a bell toll and find out a friend from another town has died. Death must reside in the other town, they decide, we must find Death and slay the monster! And so they set off, but before going too far they meet an old man whom they treat in a shabby fashion. He tells them they'll find Death under a tree in the nearby forest. And when they arrive at the tree, they find not Death, but a huge pile of gold coins. They are ecstatic but decide to wait until dark before carying the gold back home.

One of the trio is sent to get them food, and he begins to plot to keep the gold for himself. He decides to kill the other two, and he acquires some poison which he pours into two of the three bottles of wine he has bought.

Meanwhile, the other two decide *they* will share the gold themselves. When the third man returns, they engage him in horseplay, so diverting him that he doesn't see one of them draw a dagger. He is killed, and then the other two decide to celebrate. They reach for the wine the third man has brought. Each drinks a bottle quickly, and soon they truly meet Death.

The same quest, the same theme is present here as in *The Treasure of the Sierra Madre*: gold is the foundation of evil; the pursuit of material rewards is not only self-defeating but obnoxious. In effect, when we think we've succeeded, we've failed altogether.

And didn't Traven steal Chaucer's plot?

15

Ambition

Suppose we come across the true story of a simple schoolteacher living in sixteenth-century Germany who teaches in various university cities. The only unusual thing about him is his avocation: in an age of staunch religious worship and influence he likes to do magic tricks, and at times he offers to tell fortunes. He toys with the inexplicable, and in so doing he runs counter to popular belief that man should leave to God and his chosen messenger all things for which there may or may not be an answer.

As our schoolteacher travels about he is dismissed by many as a charlatan, a phony interested only in fattening his private account at the expense of the poor souls he might deceive. But then he appears in Cologne, and the archbishop has a chance to observe him and to witness his magic and his prophecies. Within days, stories of the schoolteacher's supernatural powers burst across the face of Germany, and the archbishop of Cologne becomes his patron. His reputation spreads even as the Protestant Reformation of Martin Luther gathers steam, and in fact Luther himself comes to believe in the supernatural powers of this one-time, little-respected schoolteacher. By the end of the sixteenth century he has assumed almost legendary size as the embodiment of the magic and the pseudoscience that filtered through the medieval period. Tales of what he can do are told and retold across the face of Europe.

Now, what if... we take this true story and create a piece of fiction? What if... our schoolteacher becomes a scholar deeply enmeshed in the meaning of life, aspiring to powers no other mortal possesses? His store of knowledge is vast but he recognizes that man's ability to acquire knowledge is limited. His soul needs release from earthly constraints so he can aspire to the supersensual, where he could learn the very meaning of existence. Now, since the story of the schoolteacher occurs against the background of deep religious upheaval and concern, our scholar — his life updated to a more modern era, of course — might also have to deal with a conflict that bears on religion. But let's not shroud things in dogma or practice. Instead, let's have our scholar become — the pawn in the struggle between the Devil and the Lord. In short, let's reduce the conflict to its barest, most fundamental level...

And for a story we have the famous tale of *Faust* by Johann Wolfgang von Goethe, written in the early part of the nineteenth century. Goethe's story is, in fact, the retelling of the old legend that surrounded the sixteenth-century magician and schoolteacher who also carried the name of Faust. In Goethe's story the Devil, who takes the name of Mephistopheles, makes a wager with the Lord that Faust can be tempted to renounce his beliefs and his righteous integrity. Both know that the only way this can be done is if Mephistopheles can gain control of Faust's soul. Twice, the Devil tempts Faust, but to no avail. Faust continues to search for the true meaning of life, his ambition now so profound that he renounces most of the things that make life worthwhile. There must be experience so profound, so enduring that it transcends what is available on this earth.

Okay, says Mephistopheles, if this is what you seek, and I am able to provide it, then I claim your soul.

Faust agrees.

Ambition for something unattainable to all other mortals is Faust's desire. It is ambition, without question, on the grandest scale.

Mephistopheles sets to work. First he restores Faust's youth, and then he introduces Faust to Gretchen, a pure and beautiful young woman. At first Faust vows he will not touch her because she is so innocent and unsullied. But the Devil sends her jewels which Gretchen thinks come from Faust, and Faust is then tempted to pursue his love for her, and she surrenders herself to him.

Gretchen's brother convinces her she has done a terrible wrong, and she turns in grief to Faust who decides to kill her brother.

Is his love now so overwhelming and his spirit so fulfilled that he would wish this moment to endure forever? The Devil wonders.

No, says Faust, human love, even enduring love, cannot satisfy my cravings...

Then Mephistopheles creates the living image of the most beautiful woman who has ever lived — Helen of Troy — and in presenting her to Faust hopes that now, finally, Faust will cry for the moment to stay forever.

But Faust doesn't bite. Beauty is but a passing thing, he says, it is no more lasting than any other sensual earthly experience...

And Faust shakes off further ambition for supersensual experience. He sets about producing something useful for mankind. The Devil wipes away the supernatural powers he has granted Faust and retreats, not content to give up his quest.

Many years pass and Faust has now made it possible for large numbers of people to live and work on land he has owned and to produce something useful for themselves and for mankind. At this moment he cries out for everything to stay as it is, that life is worth living and that things, as they are, should endure forever...

And Mephistopheles has him!

Or has he? Faust may have cried for a moment to endure, but has he also renounced his beliefs and righteous integrity? Apparently Goethe didn't think so because in the end the Lord dispatches angels to help Faust ascend to heaven.

Did Goethe steal his plot? Is Faust's overriding ambition so unique that Goethe is the only one who can tell it? Not at all. More than 200 years before Goethe's work, Johann Spiess produced a story *Historia von Dr. Johann Fausten* which had Faust making his deal with the Devil so he could enjoy twenty-four years of pleasure and power before his soul was to be given to the Devil. This Faust even had a sensual experience with Helen of Troy and fathered a child by her. At the end of the twenty-four years he is carried off to Hell and now deeply regrets having bartered his soul for what he claims are transitory pleasures. Then there's Christopher Marlowe's famous drama, *The Tragedy of Dr. Faustus*, written in 1589, as well as a number of other works on the same theme, including symphonies, operas, and other musical works. Did they all steal their story lines and plots?

Certainly, but the legend of Faust and the magician and fortune teller lives on. Anyone can try his hand, it seems.

Shakespeare uses the idea of ambition frequently in his work. In *Julius Caesar*, of course, it is the prime motivating factor for the action. Caesar, by far the most powerful man in Rome, now contemplates accepting the crown which would make him King, his power absolute, his decisions unquestioned. The conspirators gather because they sense an unnerving movement towards dictatorship and unreasonable authoritarianism. They strike!... and Caesar is dead, and the threat of one man's ambition dies as well. What did Shakespeare think of ambition? In the orations of Brutus and Antony at Caesar's funeral he is quite clear:

Brutus, Caesar's close friend and confidant and one of the assassins, speaks first:

> As Caesar loved me, I weep for him; as he was fortunate I rejoice in it; as he was valiant, I honour him; *but as he was ambitious*, I slew him. There is tears for his love; joy for his fortune; honour for his valour; *and death for his ambition*...

Anthony, one of Caesar's generals and a long-time compatriot on the battlefield, then speaks:

> The noble Brutus hath told you Caesar was ambitious: if it were so, it was a grevious fault... for Brutus says he was ambitious; and Brutus is an honorable man. He hath brought many captives home to Rome, whose ransoms did the general coffers fill; did this in Caesar seem ambitious? When that the poor have cried, Caesar hath wept; *ambition should be made of sterner stuff*...

The point here is that ambition, to Shakespeare, has pejorative leanings, and when someone is ambitious, that is, when they show strong interest in their own personal advancement, and especially at the expense of someone else, then obviously it is not something to be admired.

Clearly, ambition is the plot motivator for this story. Shakespeare also uses a number of story spicers. Perhaps most prominent is the use of conspiracy, the plotting of Brutus, Cassius, Casca and the others to murder Caesar. We follow the plot from Cassius's first words to Brutus and the disaffection of Casca on through the subterfuge to enlist Brutus's support, the gathering of the weapons and finally the deed itself.

Another story spicer is the use of criminal action — specifically murder — which of course enlivens the plot substantially. By its very nature political conspiracy is a traumatic event because it seeks to replace established power which has already indicated it will not be replaced. Upheaval is the natural result, and violence will follow with certainty. Imagine a political conspiracy without the threat of murder, especially two thousand years ago, and we have a plot that loses much of its tension.

Shakespeare touches on other story spicers in *Julius Caesar*. There's authority in that the conspirators are afraid Caesar wishes to extend his powers; there's deception in that Cassius plays on Brutus's fears to bring him into the conspiratorial circle, and, of course, there's Brutus's deception in turning on his friend and patron and killing him; there's honor and dishonor in the manner of Brutus's approach to the assassination and the fact that he has great respect for Caesar even after killing him. Yet Brutus, too, is held in high honor by those who know him. Note the reaction of Ligarius who encounters Brutus shortly before the assassination. He asks Brutus about his plans and Brutus replies, "A piece of work that will make sick men whole."

Ligarius wonders what that could be, and Brutus tells him he'll explain it if Ligarius wants to come along. Ligarius then says:

> Set on your foot, and with a heart new-fired I follow you, to do I know not what; but it sufficeth that Brutus leads me on . . .

The end product of ambition in political circles is power, and in *MacBeth* Shakespeare has his lead character seeking to become king of Scotland. The plot includes murder, conspiracy, treachery, dishonor — all the items that go along with the concept of political ambition realized to its extreme. Could MacBeth gain his dream of the throne without murdering the king of Scotland? Perhaps, if he had patience, but then once power is tasted, patience is often a casualty. MacBeth, spurred on by his wife, plots to kill the king and his sons, and later when he has assumed the throne and his former friend, MacDuff, has gone away to join those seeking to oust MacBeth, he kills Mac-Duff's wife and children. MacBeth also murders his friend Banquo in the course of the conspiracy, and then, finally as king, he himself becomes a target of others who wish him removed. It is the story of *Julius Caesar* carried an additional step: now the conspirators themselves have assumed the power they refused to serve.

The ambition of MacBeth is the major plot motivator in Shakespeare's work. The story, in bold outlines, is a blueprint that others have followed through the centuries, and Shakespeare's warning that oversized ambition carries with it the seeds of its own destruction is a thoroughly modern concept. Let's take just one example: a young man with political ambition is county treasurer and he fights against a corrupt building contractor who is constructing the local schoolhouse. The treasurer ends up losing his job over the conflict, but two years later the fire escape on the building collapses during a fire drill and the treasurer is vindicated.

Some years pass and the treasurer is now running for governor, his youthful vigor now replaced by a cynical opportunism. After he is elected, his political maneuvering begins on a grand scale, and his wife retreats to her sister's farm, agreeing to appear in public with him only for the sake of his reputation. He has a mistress, an assortment of strong-armed bodyguards, and an ambition to build a huge medical-center complex carrying his name.

This is the story line for Robert Penn Warren's fine work, *All The King's Men*, which won the Pulitzer Prize in 1947. Willie Stark, the Governor, is not above blackmail or conspiracy to achieve his ends, and in fact uses and misuses various people in order to maintain and solidify his position. When old Judge Irwin stands in the way of one of Willie's plans, he orders his executive assistant to delve into the judge's past and find a scandal that could be used. When Willie wants a well-respected local surgeon to become chief of the new hospital, and the surgeon turns him down, he has documents shown to the surgeon's sister which prove their father, as governor, had covered up acceptance of a bribe by Judge Irwin. When Willie tries to intimidate Judge Irwin in order to stop one of his political enemies from trying his own form of blackmail, the judge shoots himself after learning that Willie has information about the judge's acceptance of a bribe. When Willie tires of his mistress, he takes up with the sister of the surgeon who heads the new medical center.

And, finally, the surgeon, distraught about the news of his sister and Willie, confronts the governor in the hallway of the state capitol. And he shoots him.

Quite obviously there are wide differences between this work and the Shakespearean tragedies, *Julius Caesar* and *MacBeth*. Yet in each instance it is cynical political ambition turned to self-serving ends that destroys the character. Story spicers fill Robert Penn Warren's work: there's suicide and deception and conspiracy and criminal action that add substance to the basic plot motivator and show, just as Shakespeare does, that ambition provides a fertile arena within which to construct a story. Willie Stark rises to power and maintains himself by opportunism and illegality, and in the end, just as Julius Caesar and MacBeth discover, the people one uses and abuses on the way to the top will have their day.

Modern political ambition on a national scale can also be fruitful for plot motivation, though the only difference with other stories is in the setting. But ever since the late nineteen fifties the somewhat strange and intriguing stage of national politics has become more and more familiar, perhaps starting with Allen Drury's 1959 novel *Advise and Consent*. Ambition always plays a part in these works, and since it's political ambition, we're bound to see story spicers like conspiracy and criminal action and deception fill the pages. Ambition, after all, is pretty dull stuff unless it's spurred by someone doing something he or she shouldn't be doing. A good example is Gore Vidal's *Washington D.C.*, published in 1967. Though the action in the story takes place from the late nineteen thirties to the early nineteen fifties, it is a political drama that deals with ideas from any age. U.S. Senator James Burden Day is from a western oil state, and early in his career he had done a favor for an oil speculator interested in buying up Indian lands, a favor which was quite obviously illegal. Now, years later, Day wants to run for the presidency, but then Franklin Roosevelt decides on a third term and Day's ambition is stymied. His assistant, Clay Overbury, also has political ambition, but war intervenes and Overbury serves until the war ends. Then Overbury returns and runs for Congress, and several years later he confronts Senator Day about that little favor he did for the oil speculator some years back. He wants Day's senate seat, and, without being pushed, Day moves aside. At this time Overbury has also married into the Sanford family. Blaise Sanford is the publisher of a very strong and influential Washington newspaper, and he's glad to see his daughter, Enid, marry Overbury. However, Enid slowly succumbs to alcohol and other pleasures of the flesh until she is in danger of becoming a severe embarrassment for Overbury. At this point, Blaise Sanford, who has been beating the drums for Overbury in his newspaper, sees the sorrowful consequences for Overbury if the truth about Enid were made public. So he has her committed to an asylum, and then Clay Overbury is relatively free to begin his real quest — a run for the presidency of the United States.

Here, once again, we have political ambition employing the darker side of human nature to achieve its ends. There's blackmail and conspiracy and deception with but one goal in mind — the top political office. In a general sense Vidal's story mirrors both *Julius Caesar* and *MacBeth*: a conspiracy to gain a position of power, the use of underhanded, illegal, disreputable means and a dangling question of whether those means ever, *ever* justify the ends sought.

Ambition has many faces, though it ultimately translates into power, prestige, wealth, respect in some combination. Can a man aspire to be a good father? Can a tennis professional aspire to win Wimbledon? Can a cook aspire to make a perfect Hollandaise sauce? Can an oil rigger aspire to drill a hole deeper than anyone has done before?

These are the elements of a story, and as we broaden the scope of the ambition that will motivate the story, we create a story line. Now, can a man aspire to be a good father when his work takes him away most of the week or when he's suddenly confronted by obtaining custody of his children because his ex-wife doesn't want them? Can a tennis professional aspire to win Wimbledon when her marriage has just broken up or her mother is dying or her knees are deteriorating badly?

The point of all this is: how outsized is that ambition? For purposes of a good story, the more outsized the better!

Which brings us to someone whose ambition knew no bounds, none whatsoever. His name is Sammy Glick, and he came from a miserably poor section of New York, his sole aim to "better himself." In Budd Schulberg's *What Makes Sammy Run* (1941) Sammy starts off as a copyboy on a newspaper in his middle teens, and by the time he is nineteen he has become a radio columnist, even though he has no skill in writing or producing. As the author points out, Sammy's life is a continual "blitzkrieg against his fellow man," yet his ambition never wavers. With the help of a stolen manuscript he moves on to Hollywood and uses ghost writers and collaborators to promote himself. Eventually Sammy Glick — tough, unscrupulous, amoral... and unabashedly ambitious, becomes a Hollywood big-shot writer-producer. But still he can't write a line. Sammy's Hollywood wedding is an unimagined extravaganza and as the book closes Sammy becomes — finally — the head of a major studio.

Even though *What Makes Sammy Run* is sometimes called a "Hollywood" novel, it's actually the story of a man's rise in the business world, in this case the business of movie-making. A business setting is a good story forum for ambition as a plot motivator. After all, business and money go together, and if one aspires for wealth, prestige and power, what better way than at the top of the business heap? To be ambitious in the business world is to be expected, it is part of the business ethic. Few business people enter the battle without ambition, and that ambition can form the core of a good story. Sometimes ambition can run amuck, as with Sammy Glick. Sometimes its urgings are more subtle, though the consequences can be equally disagreeable.

In John P. Marquand's *Sincerely Willis Wayde*, published in 1955, we start with a young man, idealistic, interested in the beauty of nature and the outdoors. At age fifteen Willis Wayde and his family move to Clyde, Massachusetts where Willis's father, Alfred Wayde, an itinerant engineer from the western United States, is hired by Henry Harcourt, owner of the Harcourt Mill, to help rejuvenate the mill. This is during the Depression, and with Alfred Wayde's help, the mill and then the town are able to survive the bad years. During this time Willis becomes drawn to Bess Harcourt, Henry Harcourt's granddaughter, and to Henry Harcourt himself. He tries to emulate the old man — his elegant style, his clothes, his knowledge of antiques, the ease with which he manages people. Willis then goes off to college and finally to Harvard Business School, and we see the idealistic young man slowly become transformed into an ambitious businessman. He becomes very important to the mill itself, and then he gets additional training in New York as an industrial consultant. By this time Henry Harcourt is dead, and his granddaughter, Bess, owns the mill.

He asks Bess to sell him the mill, intending to combine it with another business in the first of a series of conglomerates he will create. Bess will sell him the mill, but she assumes, because of their early years together and his love for the mill and the town, that he will protect them and the jobs of those who work there. Two months later, after the mill is his, he closes it down. In short order Willis becomes a wealthy businessman, and by now he is totally devoted to the business way of life. Yet try as he might, he can never recapture the elegance and the style of Henry Harcourt. He wants to become a businessman with social responsibility, but the latter role eludes him completely. "I've tried to be sincere," he tells his wife, Sylvia, "I really have. But sometimes it's a problem, how to be sincere."

As he continues to try and follow in Henry Harcourt's steps, he begins to study up on antiques. But once again he falls on his face. His motivation has no substance. "The heads of a great many businesses seem to collect antiques," he says, "They're apt to appreciate someone who knows about them."

In the end it's Bess Harcourt who categorizes Willis Wayde properly. After she learns what he did with the Harcourt Mill once he owned it, she calls him a Uriah Heap.

And who is Uriah Heap? In Charles Dickens's *David Copperfield* he is the despicable little character who starts as a clerk in a law office, worms his way into the confidence of his employer, becomes a partner in the firm, ruins the man who gave him his chance and then embezzles some money — all the time insisting he is a very humble and undeserving person.

Maybe John P. Marquand didn't steal his plot from Charles Dickens, but stealing a character is the next best thing.

Ambition as a plot motivator gives a fertile image to many story ideas. One an be ambitious in politics... in love... in athletics... in business... in war... in science. The settings for a story where ambition plays an important role are as endless as the variety of stories themselves. Ambition as the ardent urge for personal advancement is the key to stories where such craving lifts the character (or characters) from the pack and makes him (or them) outsized, different, memorable.

PART THREE
To Steal or Not to Steal

16

Plagiarism and Copyright

"My first published novel was very clearly an imitation of Henry James," says a world-reknowned fiction writer without a trace of discomfort.

"Six sentences were taken..." another best-selling writer admits when he is charged with plagiarizing. "Omission of the source was an oversight of the typist."

Both writers freely acknowledge they have taken something original from someone else. In one case it's perfectly acceptable, in the other case, it's not. What's the difference?

Plot, plot, plot... stealing a plot is like capturing a breath of air. It's there for our use — no one can own it forever. But stealing someone else's words — no!

Some years ago we came across a short story about two people who burglarize an establishment and get away with a bundle. Later they argue about how to divide the loot, and each, without the knowledge of the other, poisons something the other is about to swallow. The famous author had copyrighted his story, and sometime later a movie studio produced a movie with a strikingly similar plot line. The author sued for copyright infringement, claiming his original idea had been stolen.

Not so, said a federal judge. "The plot is highly dramatic and calculated to appeal powerfully to reader or spectator. But it is an old one..." The judge traced the plot back to Chaucer's *Pardonner's Tale* (and its offspring, *The Treasure of Sierra Madre*, mentioned in chapter fourteen). Then he added, "The plot is common property; no one, by presenting it with modern incidents, can appropriate it by copyrighting."

If this isn't plagiarism, just exactly what is it? The simple answer is that you have to steal something "original" from someone else before they'll call you a plagiarist. But to decide *that* we first have to figure out what is meant by "originality."

Let's clear up something right away. Plagiarism and copyright have a lot to do with each other, but they aren't the same thing at all. Plagiarism is the act of stealing something original... copyright is the act of protecting something original. When we copyright an original work, it's as if we've put an umbrella over it, and the only time we'll remove that umbrella — even briefly — will be to give someone else permission to use our original thoughts. No one can use them without our permission. No one.

That doesn't mean they won't try. A plagiarist is someone who steals without attribution, without credit, without conscience. The literary annals are full of tales of inventive pilfering, and over the centuries the courts have fashioned a body of law that strives to keep things in check.

How original do we have to be? History shows us it's really a matter of degree. Homer had a vast store of legends and myths to draw from in his Aegean world, and his *Iliad* and *Odyssey* were faithful representations of those myths and legends.

But... it was the *way* he told his tales, his creative organizing of disparate pieces that turned them into a coherent whole. Vergil, the greatest Roman poet of them all, copied the story of the fall of Troy from Pisander and patterned his love idyll of Aeneas and Dido carefully on that of Medea and Jason, in the work of Apollonius. Vergil, too, followed Homer quite closely arranging army formations, setting up funeral games, even to having his hero almost succumb to the seductive offerings of a temptress. Alexander Lindey quotes Auden as saying, "Vergil's conscious imitation of Homer is, of course, not due to lack of invention; indeed, it is often precisely when he copies most closely that the novelty of his vision is clearest. The *Iliad* is poetry of the highest order, but it is the poetry of barbarians, of a tribal culture; The *Aeneid* is the poetry of civilization, of world history. A child can enjoy Homer; anyone who has come to appreciate Vergil has already grown up."

The giants of the literary scene through the ages were not above plot-purloining if it served their creative purposes. Plato, Horace, Dante, Chaucer, Edmund Spenser, Milton — the list could go on and on. Even Shakespeare — particularly Shakespeare — used everything he could find, from Greek biography to Roman history to long-forgotten legends. But Shakespeare also did a bit of paraphrasing, that seemingly innocuous description which can be a dangerous bridge into plagiarism. Just check this description of the ideal state...

> I' the commonwealth, I would by contraries
> Execute all things; for no kind of traffic,
> Would I admit; no name of magistrate;
> Letters should not be known; no use of service
> Of riches or of poverty; no contracts,
> Succession; bound of land; tilth, vinyard, none;
> No use of metal, corn or wine, or oil;
> No occupation; all men, all.
> — Shakespeare (*The Tempest*)

...with the words of Michel de Montaigne, written a quarter of a century, or more, before...

> It is a nation (would I answer Plato) that hath no kind of traffic, no knowledge of letters, no intelligence of number, no name of magistrate, nor of politic superiority, no use of service, or riches, or of poverty; no contracts, no successions, no occupations, but idle... nor no jug of wine, corn or metal...

Sure, it's plagiarism of a sort, but so what? It's the way Shakespeare handled his story that's crucial, and if we can see the seeds of his own originality, then a few words that parallel a few words of someone else's is nothing to get excited about. But just remember, every writer owes his originality to another. We're all the products of what has been written before us, and we use and reuse plots, characters, incidents, treatments that others have dramatized over and over. And it's okay.

Originality, then, is the key to plagiarism. If we copy out words verbatim without attribution, and we publish them as our own, we've stolen them. Simple as that. We've plagiarized, we've broken the law. Of course, the copying must be more than incidental, not just a couple of words or phrases, even though, technically, whatever is taken is thought of as plagiarizing.

The courts aren't looking to punish the nibblers — they want those who take big bites, those who pilfer on a grand scale. Take, for example, the concerns of an unhappy gentleman named Suid. Some years back he wrote a 357-page book, *Guts and Glory — Great American War Movies*. Of course, the war hero's war hero, John Wayne, had a starring role in the book, and there were interviews with various producers, directors and quotes from others who had been active in the war-movie field.

Along comes *Newsweek* Magazine and publishes an article, "John Wayne: End as a Man." Suid reads the article and finds there are some quotes taken from his book — a portion of one of

Wayne's unpublished letters, portions of a couple of interviews with other war-movie buffs, portions of an unpublished letter by Jack Valenti, portions of two quotes from a book by Ron Kovics — six specific items in all.

The judge wasn't impressed with Suid's arguments. Sure, there was copying, even paraphrasing, and verbatim reproduction of a historical or factual work is against the law. But here it was really just nibbling; the material on John Wayne made up only two chapters in the book, a very small part. "However, there was not sufficient copying or paraphrasing in this case to constitute wholesale appropriation," the judge concluded. *Newsweek* wins.

Basic protection from the plagiarizer is the copyrighting of what it is we've created. To copyright means to announce publicly that we've produced something original and that anyone who wants to use it or any portion of it had better be careful not to take our original thoughts or ideas or treatment and claim them as their own.

There are two forms of copyright — common-law and statutory. Common-law copyright is something that has come along through the centuries as a device to protect the first level of originality — our unpublished creative product. It provides an author an exclusive and perpetual right in all of his *unpublished* works. It means that each of us can sell, or license others to use, anything we have written *just because we have written it*! It may never have been published, but that doesn't matter. It is ours, and our heirs', to do with as we and they choose, and no one else can lay claim to it for any reason. If Great-grandfather had written a bawdy novel in the nineteenth century, and it had never been published, and we were his rightful heirs... we could publish it today as our own under our common-law copyright. This right never ceases, so long as the work is not published and made available to the general public.

When that happens, the common-law copyright stops! It evaporates.

But protection is still available. Now the emphasis is on statutory copyright. Just like common-law copyright this is exclusive, but it doesn't attach to our work like some free-flying particle. Statutory copyright is what we are granted by the government to prevent others from copying our work. It protects work from the day it is published, provided we have applied for the copyright under the statute. It gives us the sole right to publish and make copies of our works, to record them and perform them *for a limited period of time*. Note this again — a limited period of time!

We get a statutory copyright by publishing our work, and it remains effective for fifty years after our death. A new copyright law went into effect on January 1, 1978 which set up this fifty-year duration (and it now also includes all the rights we used to have under common-law copyright). But for all works published before January 1, 1978, we're still governed by the old law. That provided a statutory copyright for only twenty-eight years with a renewal permitted for another forty-seven years.

Under either law, however, our copyright gives us certain exclusive rights. We, and only we, can:

1. Reproduce the copyrighted work in copies or phono-records
2. Prepare derivative works based upon the copyrighted work
3. Authorize distribution, sale, rental, lease or lending of copies
4. Authorize the public performance of the work
5. Authorize the public display of the work

The purpose of statutory copyright is to provide notice to all that we have created and published an original work and that anyone copying from it and presenting it as their own is violating the law. The statute also allows us to register the work with the Copyright Office in Washington. This is called "copyright registration," and while it isn't essential for copyright protection, it is essential if we need to file a copyright-infringement suit because someone else has stolen our work. An infringement suit is the legal action we take against someone who violates our copyright. It asserts that the violators must be ordered to stop infringing and that we are entitled to damages. But, even if our suit is successful, we can't collect damages or attorney fees for any period during which infringement took place up to the moment of registration.

Having copyright registration gives pretty complete protection. It provides notice, especially of a claim to original work. Someone could argue, for example, they didn't know our work was copyrighted because there was no notice of it in the work. If we hadn't registered with the Copyright Office, they might get away with it. But anyone can check with that office, and many do, so there is no basis for a claim of ignorance here.

How and where do we register?

Get a Copyright Information Kit from the Copyright Office, Library of Congress, Washington, D.C. 20559. It includes regulations, registration forms, explanation sheets and a copy of the current law. Just follow the directions.

Just exactly what can be copyrighted? The statute is pretty clear. Literary, dramatic, musical, pictorial, graphic, sculptural and choreographic works can be copyrighted. Pantomime, films, audio-visual materials and sound-recordings are also included. Anything, in fact, that is an "original work of authorship" portrayed in a "tangible medium of expression."

What about something somebody says? Oral communication later put in writing? Would that fit here?

How about the words of Ernest Hemingway — not his written words but his oral communication? Dialogue he had with a young, aspiring writer that the young writer taped over a period of time?

Of course the words are copyrightable! Hemingway's heirs said. The great man's contributions to these conversations were unique and amounted to literary compositions in themselves. No one can print them without our permission.

Phooey! said the young writer. A conversation is never a one-sided affair. Two people contribute to it, and who's to say that the pearls dropping from one person's lips aren't evoked or produced by the other's comments? I selected and compiled these conversations. I set them in proper order so we could have a coherent story.

But these are Hemingway's *words*, the heirs protested.

And this is *my* treatment of them, the young author responded.

Correct! echoed the court. "Conversations... are inevitably the product of interaction between the parties; they are not individual intellectual productions."

The young author wins. The only literary-property right available here goes to the writer, not the speaker.

Suppose we wake up one morning and discover our favorite piece of creative work has been plagiarized. What do we do?

Assuming it was copyrighted, we head for a good lawyer, and we file a copyright-infringement lawsuit. We claim our original work has been infringed upon by the unscrupulous plagiarizer, and we demand damages in the form of all profits the plagiarizer has pocketed and an injunction to stop him (or her) from doing this in the future.

But we have to prove the plagiarism, and sometimes that's not so easy. It's our burden since we are the one who is complaining. Suppose we write a book about the life of Jesus Christ, casting him as a cynical conniver bent on bringing out the Old Testament prophecies concerning the coming of a Messiah — himself, in fact — and that he plans to simulate his death on the Cross through a drug-induced trance (which would then allow him magically to "resurrect himself" when the drug wears off).

We conclude by having the plan cruelly foiled because a clumsy Roman soldier doesn't follow the script and ends up killing him. We read in the local paper that someone else has put together a rock opera called *Jesus Christ Superstar*, about a charismatic rock-and-roll singer who sees himself as the perfect roll player for Jesus on the Cross. But in the end his outsized ego actually forces him to die on the Cross.

Our antennae spring into action. There are similarities, parallelisms as both works try to humanize and politicize Jesus even as they scandalize the conventional religious believers. The works are grounded on the character of Jesus, his historical setting and, of course, his religious experiences. In other words, the plot of our book has been stolen.

But has our original treatment been stolen, too? Has our copyright been infringed?

The author of the first book is Dr. Hugh J. Schofield, and he wrote *The Passover Plot* some years ago, attempting to depict Jesus as a high-minded conniver intent on bringing about the coming of a Messiah. The book is copyrighted, and the question — does the rock opera *Jesus Christ Superstar* infringe on the copyright of *The Passover Plot*?

The judge looked carefully at both works but concluded there was no copyright infringement and, thus, no plagiarism. "Similarity of incidents, alone, will not constitute an infringement," he said, "especially when both works are based on common sources and concern events in the life of an historical figure." But the differences were significant items: the book had no musical score, it could be read and enjoyed without any musical accompaniment, it deals with the entire life of Jesus (the opera concentrates only on the last seven days), the opera's message comes through the music and the libretto, and it really contains no "book" in the customary broadway-musical sense.

The moral's pretty clear: steal a plot, steal a character, steal an historical time frame, steal, even, a new look at an old event.

common-law copyright? They are perpetual and attach from the moment the work is finished, *regardless of whether it is ever published*. There's no public domain to worry about with common-law copyright.

And wouldn't Mark Twain laugh at that! Mark Twain, it seems, came up with an idea that if several writers took a common plot and wrote different portions of the story, it could make a most interesting result. Twain's idea blossomed in 1876. (Almost one hundred years later, a group of *Newsday* Long Island newspapermen decided to do the same thing and to write an admittedly erotic novel, *Naked Came the Stranger*, with each one donating a chapter. The putative author was Penelope Ash.)

Mark Twain put together an outline which contained the story line of the book, but the outline was not intended for publication. He submitted the outline to a national magazine, but it was rejected. And Twain went on to other things.

Some fifty-five years later — twenty years after Twain died — a copy of the outline surfaced, and an enterprising chap announced that he would publish it. The ballyhoo was poised — Mark Twain lives! The man who gave us Tom Sawyer and Huckleberry Finn now gives us a memorable experience a generation after he has died!

Oh no, said Twain's executors. The literary rights in that little outline belong to us. Whatever the master created, from the moment his pen hit paper, is protected by common-law copyright. An outline is still a creative product. No public domain here. The rights belong to us.

And the court agreed. The physical manuscript belongs to the person who is holding it. But the literary rights to that manuscript belong to the author or his representatives. Common-law copyright, don't you see?

So much for Mark Twain.

But, then, there are times when, copyright notwithstanding, we can take from someone's work, and no one will give a damn!

We can "plagiarize" and the author, his publisher, the courts and even the policy of the United States won't raise an objection. For under the heading of "fair use," quoting a limited number of words of original work is permissible to illustrate a point. Such use is considered "fair" as long as it doesn't expropriate too much or go into great detail.

Who falls under the umbrella of fair use? We all do. Copyright protection is really a sweeping monopoly, and through the generations there has been grumbling about such a restrictive practice in a society based on competition. Monopolies in our democratic structure are insulated from the pressures of competition, and to attach a monopoly to something that each of us competes for — original thoughts and ideas — is to give an unfair advantage.

The other side of it is that the monopoly is limited in time and encourages original expression because of the rewards that might be there. The Supreme Court echoes this. "The sole interest of the United States and the primary object in conferring the monopoly lie in the general benefits derived by the public from the labors of authors." The monopoly is supposed to promote all this.

But the occasional grumbling persists. So, the idea of fair use is a way to limit the pervasiveness of the monopoly. It's well recognized, too. If we are a critic and we want to write reams about a new novel, we can quote it or paraphrase from it pretty much at will; if we are a newsperson and an original piece of work has suddenly become news (a step-by-step escalation towards nuclear war, for example, which foretells events that are actually transpiring), extensive summarizing or paraphrasing or even quoting would be okay; if we take an original work and parody it, using some of the same language and ideas, this would also be fair use; if we are a teacher or involved in research and make copies in pursuit of our purpose to educate and/or learn, there shouldn't be a problem.

But where we research and lift out copyrighted material and

publish and don't attribute, there *is* a problem. Fair use means limited use, and so long as we aren't using someone else's original work to give a special charge to our own original work, there's usually little problem. A sentence or two is okay, maybe an entire paragraph, but anything longer than this should carry the permission of the copyright holder. Certainly it would be questionable to use, without permission, an original treatment, or someone else's fictional characters — unless these things are in the public domain or we use them for the limited purposes outlined above. And if what we use adds significantly to our own work, then there's probably some big trouble ahead.

That's what the Meeropol brothers tried to pin on lawyer Louis Nizer, author of *The Implosion Conspiracy* which appeared in 1973. Nizer's book was about the espionage trial of Julius and Ethel Rosenberg, convicted of passing atomic secrets to the Russians in the early 1950s. The Rosenbergs were sentenced to death, and while they were in prison, they wrote a number of letters to their young sons — 29 letters in all — portions of which were quoted in Nizer's book.

The Meeropols who happened to be the Rosenberg sons objected to these letters' appearing in print. Not because their privacy was invaded but because Nizer didn't ask their permission before including them in his book.

These letters and the literary-property right they contain belong to us! The Meeropols complained. How can Nizer use them when we're the ones who hold the copyright?

True enough, Nizer admitted, but what we're dealing with is a matter of historical significance. The public has a right to know what went on; there is strong public interest at stake.

Nizer used someone else's words!

Only to illustrate the historical facts...

And the judge agreed. Nizer didn't capitalize on the "unique intellectual product" of the person writing the letters, and the letters themselves form only a small part of the book. Nizer is entitled to "fair use" of these letters.

The judge, also, took a swipe at the monopoly aspect of the copyright, indicating that, at least in this case, in any conflict between our right to know something and our right to sit on a "unique intellectual product," he'd come down squarely on the public's right to know. "Given the public interest in the trial and the events surrounding it," the judge tells us, "plaintiffs' (the Meeropol brothers') copyright should not have given them a monopoly on the use and dissemination of facts relating to this historical event."

Nizer and fair-use win.

The newest Copyright Act brings in a category which has been treated in a nebulous way at best in the past. This is the so-called work for hire, and it adds an exception to the idea that the author always owns the copyright to his work. It concerns someone who works for someone else and produces something *in the course of his employment*.

"I want you to write a history of the company," the boss says one day, or. . .

"We need a skit for the President's birthday party. Write one, *but keep it funny!*" or. . .

"You can't put a book out using those newspaper columns you've written for the paper, without permission!" the boss says. "Those pieces were done on our time."

Works made for hire, all three. And the copyright belongs to the employer. The boss. It may contain our creative jewels and our unique intellectual product, but we probably wouldn't have put it together without our employer's instigation, and, in fact, what we've produced is exactly what we're being paid to produce anyway.

Note above that the first two instances are works "specially ordered and commissioned." The third instance is not. If we haven't signed some writtten agreement that provides for works "specially ordered and commissioned" to be called "works for hire," when they are not. It means, therefore, that we, as the author, can claim the copyright. But if we've agreed to call what we produce a "work for hire" then the boss owns the copyright.

Practically speaking, of course, if we're working for a salary and our job includes writing and producing original material for and on behalf of the company, no employer with any brains would let us get through the first day without signing something that treats our entire work product as a "work for hire." The closer call would probably occur if we are hired to produce a single work or to work for a limited period and for a limited purpose. Here again, we would be commissioned to do a specific piece of work, and the question of whether it would become a "work for hire" is something to negotiate about. Just remember this — anything which can be called a "work for hire" under the Copyright Act loses us, the author, the copyright. The boss just stuffs it into his own pocket.

Even as we wind our way through the Copyright Act, the important word to keep in mind is *originality*. That is what we're trying to protect, and that is what is so attractive to plagiarizers. Originality of expression, of treatment, of representation. Each of us has a uniqueness that makes us special targets for those who would capitalize on it. Sometimes we are the last ones to see and understand that uniqueness...

Which is what happened to a modest man named Rubin who spent years pursuing his PhD in social psychology. He wrote a dissertation on "The Social Psychology of Romantic Love" and as is customary had it copyrighted. Included in the dissertation are a "love scale" and a "liking scale," designed to elicit and measure feelings between a man and a woman.

Maybe it helps to take the guesswork out, who knows? But whatever the reason, *Boston Magazine* got hold of the scales and editorial eyes lit up like high-voltage laser beams.

The magazine published an article "ooo-ooo-wah, ooo-ooo-wah, why do fools fall in love?" The love- and like-scales were set forth prominently, and then the bottom line for it all:

"The Test of Love" in a box for the readers to play with. does she love me, does she not? Does he love me, does he not?

Dr. Rubin certainly didn't love — or like — *Boston Magazine*. My love- and like-scales are my original, creative work, he said. You have infringed my copyright.

Rubbish! scoffed the magazine. What you produced was a scientific discovery. Everyone knows that's not copyrightable. Original, your work may be, but no literary-property right is involved in it.

The scales are an original form of expression, Dr. Rubin insisted...

The magazine disagreed. Our purpose in publishing the scales was to acquaint the public with the available scientific research in a topic that's certainly of interest to us all. It's a scientifically exciting discovery.

You used my research to sell more magazines, Dr. Rubin grumbled. Your purpose was commercial, not altruistic...

How true! the court said. Dr. Rubin's scales had copyrighted protection — they are an original work with a literary-property right. Originality is to be protected above all. (If we read between the lines here, we can see another reason for the judge's decision: *Boston Magazine* capitalized on its plagiarism; it's motive was strictly commercial. The magazine might have argued the idea of "fair use" because the scales really weren't that large a portion of the article. But when more magazines are sold because of what has been stolen, fair use doesn't become so fair anymore.)

Originality, then, is the name of the game. But even the Copyright Act recognizes that an original work doesn't blossom out of the air, the framework is often based on something that went before it. There is even a section in the Act for copyrighting "derivative work." This means, simply, a work "based on one or more pre-existing works." Translations are included here, as are fictionalizations, abridgements, condensations or "any other form in which a work may be recast, transformed or adapted." A play from a movie? Certainly... a television show from a play? Of course... a book from a magazine article? Yes... any type of original treatment, in other words, that makes it a unique intellectual product.

However, work created by lifting out someone else's words, phrases and sentences is not derivative, nor is it a unique intellectual product. It is a plagiarism.

This is what Jacob Epstein found out not long after he published his first book, *Wild Oats*, in 1979. Epstein wrote his book during his senior year at Yale, and it was published shortly after he graduated. It is the story of Billy Williams, and the first three months of his life at a last-chance liberal arts institution, Beacham University. Billy has asthma, insomnia, a roommate from Los Angeles who utters "so fine!" to almost anything and a mother who worships the memory of Bobby Kennedy and is about to get married for the third time. This is also the story of Billy and Zizi Zanzibar, a far-out coed, who spins his sensibilities about like a top and has been impregnated by Billy's literature professor. Billy is full of the ineffective yearnings for maturity that all quasi-adults have, he wants to be thought of as a respectable mind wrapped in a respectable body, but somehow it just doesn't come out that way. At one point Billy decides to take Chinese so he can know "something hardly anyone else knew except for several hundred million Chinese," and at another time he stares at his reflection in the mirror but "sees no clues at all about what is going on inside."

Billy, of course, is an updated, slightly older version of that adolescent-to-end-all-adolescents, Holden Caulfield, and *Wild Oats* is an attempt to bridge the generations between *Catcher in the Rye* and the next line of march. One reviewer calls Billy a cross between Holden Caulfield and Woody Allen, and there's some truth in that. Billy is rarely the hero of anything, he's just a struggling post-adolescent in a not altogether friendly world. Sometimes he wins, but mostly he loses.

The reviews of the book were good, and Billy was hailed as something of a guidon for the new generation.

But that's all over now. Jacob Epstein, the author, can take little solace in the strong reviews, the kudos, the predictions of good things to come. For he's been called a plagiarizer, and he really should have known better than to let himself get into this position. His family are literary people, and at the time the book came out his father was a vice-president of a large publishing house, and his mother was an editor at the *New York Review of Books*. So the question of what he should have known looms very, very big.

Martin Amis certainly thought so. For him, what Epstein should have known was quite simple: if you pilfer words and phrases and images from another's work, you stand a damn good chance of being caught.

Martin Amis, we find out, is the son of novelist Kingsley Amis, and *he* wrote a first novel in 1973 called *The Rachael Papers*. It, too, is about a post-adolescent in school and trying to solve the dilemma of becoming a man. Here we have Charles Highway in London at cram school for 3 months (the same length of time as in Epstein's novel) in preparation for entering Oxford. He writes in his diary, keeps files and folders of notes on things he has done or wants to do, always searching to see what kind of grown-up he'll be. Like Billy Williams and his Zizi Zanzibar, Charles has his Rachael, and after meeting her and becoming smitten he prepares a careful campaign to seduce her, something almost akin to a war plan. He notes everything, including the color and consistency of used handkerchiefs, who has wrinkles, the smells in his room, the peculiarity of body functions. In short, he reports on the mystical *outside* world that he is encountering for the first time, and like Billy Williams his observations run from the ludicrous to simple bad taste. He finally loses interest in Rachael, for instance, when he finds that she wets the bed at night, has pimples and — grossness upon grossness — *evacuates her bowels*! Charles is really an Anglisized version of Billy Williams, and here may have lain the difficulty.

Because in October, 1980 Martin Amis accused Jacob Epstein of plagiarizing from *The Rachael Papers*. He cited more than 50 items that he claimed were stolen and used in *Wild Oats*, and he then listed them. Among them was a description of a balding man:

> *Epstein:* "two gray-colored wiry wings on either side of his otherwise hairless head..."
>
> *Amis:* "two grey-colored wirey wings on either side of his hairfree head..."

Amis joked that at least Epstein had changed the spelling a bit. And if this had been all there was, it probably wouldn't have mattered very much. Because, Amis admitted, "that bit about 'wiry wings' was stolen by me from Dickens."

But there were many, many more instances, Amis felt, and this could not go unchallenged. "My own feeling was largely one of embarrassment," Amis said, "I am no real admirer of my own first novel... It shamed me to see sentences exhumed for reinspection 10 years on. But something had to be done."

And something was done. Amis wrote a letter to the *London Observer* detailing each instance of the plagiarism that he believed Epstein had committed. "Epstein wasn't influenced by *The Rachael Papers*," Amis charged, "he had it flattened out beside his typewriter."

For Epstein it was high noon on the literary battlefield, and his reaction was to admit that he did in fact do some of what Amis said he did.

But it was inadvertent, he claimed, a sort of blind-flying copy exercise. "I did not realize until June, 1979," Epstein responded in the *Observer* to Amis's charge, "when I returned to New York for the publication of *Wild Oats* and one evening got down a carton of old papers and notebooks, that certain phrases and images in my novel, which I thought were original, or had been adapted from other sources into my own language, come verbatim, or nearly verbatim, from *The Rachael Papers*."

Epstein, apparently, would copy into notebooks phrases and images and passages he had read and greatly admired "to see how writers got things to work." Amis wasn't his only source. He also filled his notebooks with the words of Nabokov, Turgenev and Goethe, among others. As he wrote and rewrote, the phrases of the masters began to blend with his own words until "I believed I had synthesized so many disparate elements into my story that, in the synthesis, I'd made everything my own."

Indeed he had. Here are some samples:

Amis: "I could feel, gradually playing on my features a look of queasy hope."

Epstein: "He could feel, playing across his face, a look of queasy hope."

Amis: "My legs started off, at first spastically shooting out in all directions, then coordinating into a spastic shuffle."

Epstein: "Billy started toward her, legs spastically shooting out in all directions, then coordinating into a spastic shuffle."

Amis: "I wished she would go. I couldn't feel anything with her there. I wished she would go and let me mourn in peace."

Epstein: "He wished that she would go. He couldn't feel anything with her there. He wished she would go and let him mourn in peace."

More than fifty instances of this sort of thing occurred, according to Martin Amis (Epstein claims the number is much smaller). But clearly it's plagiarism, and its impact isn't lessened just because Epstein may have been more careless than judicious. Though Epstein was able to cut out some of the passages from the second printing, there were still many thousands of copies in distribution with the original words.

And it certainly didn't help that Epstein's plot followed the route taken by Amis. In fact, it's pretty clear that Epstein *did* steal Amis's plot. (We know he admitted to having read *The Rachael Papers*.) Three months in the lives of two young men; both away at school, sexual encounters and promiscuity; preoccupation with biological functions, ludicrous coping with the urge for self-respect and adulthood; first serious love relationship...

But stealing a plot — as we well know by now — won't bring the roof down (except when it's combined with stealing words, phrases, passages and images). Amis wasn't concerned about the plot-stealing aspect. "These parallels worried me not at all," he said. "So far as mainstream fiction is concerned, plots are awkward, limited things and belong in a common pool."

And Jacob Epstein — what was his final reaction? "There is nothing more I can say except that I regret what has happened."

17

Answers to Some Questions

We're at a writer's conference, and we've gone through some heady talk about ideas and deadlines and editors and agents and paperback rights, important things to be sure when we want to get a book published. Published writers mingle with novices, there are questions, questions, questions about the *process* of writing. How is it done? How do *you* do it?

"I write in the morning," a children's-book writer says.

"I write in the afternoon," a mystery writer says. "I'm just not a morning person."

"How many hours do you write in a day?"

Several of the published writers look at one another and smile. They know that writing can't be summed up so easily. "I probably write about sixteen hours a day," an older writer says, with the hint of a smile. "I mean, that's about the time each day that I'm giving my attention to my profession. Actually putting words on paper? Maybe three or four hours a day, but that's just the mechanical act of spewing out my creative juices."

"How do you know what to write *about*?" someone else is asked.

"Write about what you know best," comes the simple answer. "Don't fake it. Your readers will know."

"Where will I get stories from? I haven't lived a very exciting life..."

"But you're the only one who has lived your life."

"Of course."

"Think about your life, or the lives of other people you know well. Somewhere in there is a story. I guarantee it."

"Really!"

"Guaranteed."

And so we come to our story. We have a plot, we have an idea. But we wonder. Is it really ours, how much of it can we use, whose permission must we get?

"Steal a plot, any plot..." we hear the published writers emphasize. "Steal *this* plot!"

"I have so many questions, I'm just not sure..."

The writers smile and nod. "Ask anybody. Ask anything!"

So we do:

Question: What kind of plots are best?
Answer: The ones we are most familiar with. Would we write about growing up Catholic when we weren't even baptized a Catholic? Would we write about the Lower East Side of New York when we spent most of our life in the upper Midwest? Would we write about the steel industry when we've been a farmer all our life?

Question: Can we stop anyone from using a plot?
Answer: It depends. If the plot depicts us in such a way that we are easily recognizable, and especially if it holds us up to ridicule

or embarrassment, our privacy has probably been invaded, and we may be entitled to payment for damages. But — and this is a BIG but — we have to suffer injury first before we can sue. We aren't injured until the offensive material has been published. Then and only then has our right to privacy been invaded. While the plot has been brewing in the author's head and readied for publication, there's been no injury. Publication is what makes the injury tangible. Most courts wouldn't go along with stopping publication ahead of time. That is a serious burden on the First Amendment, called "prior restraint" or "censorship." So, the way we stop people from using a plot is to warn them that we'll sue if it gets into print and our privacy has been invaded. Otherwise we've got to wait until the deed is done.

Question: What if the details of the plot are so unique that we and only we fit the characterizations?
Answer: That's a rare situation, but it could happen. Assuming we weren't a public figure and therefore subject to different standards, once again we could claim privacy was invaded, *even* if the author changed our name, our description and our sex. If what we were involved in was unique, then it probably wouldn't matter what the author did. Using us and our situation in any way would cause problems. But even so — one thing writers have is imagination, so it shouldn't be hard to rearrange things sufficiently, removing the problem.

Queston: A friend told me the most wonderful story recently, and I'd like to use it as the basis for a novel. Can I do it without his permission?
Answer: If we change names and circumstances enough so no one could recognize the characters we can steal the story line and turn it into anything we like.

Question: What if I'd like to keep some of the more pertinent details?

Answer: We run the risk of being sued for invasion of privacy. Or even libel, if some of the things we write injure a person's reputation. Better to change things around and save the headaches. After all, the plot is still there!

Question: Just exactly what is invasion of privacy?
Answer: Every one of us has a right to withhold ourself from public scrutiny if we wish. We don't have to be victimized by unwarranted publicity. That's called our *right* to privacy, and whenever someone breaches it — either by photographing us, filming us, taping us or writing about us without our permission — that's an *invasion* of privacy. For example, if a newspaper published a photo of a woman struck by a vehicle and lying on the pavement with her skirt up around her hips, that would be considered an invasion of her privacy. It would certainly hold her up to embarrassment. Now, if that same woman were photographed on the pavement but not in an embarrassing pose, there would be no invasion of privacy. That would be a legitimate news item.

Question: How does an invasion of privacy differ from libel?
Answer: Libel is essentially defamation. When what we write defames someone, either because we accuse them of having committed a crime or because we hold them up to scorn and ridicule for the way they live or work or act, we have libelled them. Now, the real question comes when what we write is the truth because truth *is* a defense to libel (whereas with invasion of privacy, truth is irrelevant. If someone's privacy has been invaded, it doesn't matter that the account was truthful.) When we write truthful words about someone, and they happen to drip with scorn or venom, normally there's no libel. But, when we write truth, and there's a malicious motive behind our writing — when, for example, our real motive is to destroy their business or their reputation — that's different. Then, even though what we write might be truthful, we still have a prob-

lem. So long as our motives are pure when we write, so long as what we write is the truth, libel isn't a major difficulty. But if our words are false or inaccurate and they cause injury, then we're in trouble. Invasion of privacy refers to our right to be left alone. Libel refers to our right not to have bad things written about us. Plots which infringe on either right must be considered very carefully.

Question: Can two people really develop the same story line independently? Isn't that just too much coincidence?

Answer: Listen to what Oliver Wendell Holmes said more than a century ago: "Literature is full of coincidences, which some love to believe are plagiarisms. There are thoughts always abroad in the air which it takes more than wit to avoid hitting upon." When La Bruyere, the seventeenth-century French essayist was informed that his observations had been taken from Horace and Boileau, he responded, "I take your word for it, but I said it on my own. May I not have the same thoughts after them as others have after me?"

Question: If anyone can steal a plot, shouldn't we be careful whom we discuss our story ideas with?

Answer: Most professional writers worry about this sort of thing. We know a mystery-suspense writer, for example, who will not talk about a story idea he wants to develop until he gets assurance from the people he's speaking with that they won't use what they hear. That's going a bit far, but the thing to remember is this: we divulge our ideas at our peril!

Question: Suppose we wanted to steal the plot from a movie. Could we do it?

Answer: Of course.

Question: Or from a play or from a television show or from oral history?

Answer: Of course.

Question: If we use "what if...", where should the major changes in the old plot be made?

Answer: Start with time — should it be the present or in the past or future? Then the setting — should it be in the city or the country, the United States or somewhere else, based on a true event or not, among rich people or poor people? Then the motivators — should the same ones be used? What would happen if others were used, if other story spicers were used, as well? Then the point of view — should the story run in the same direction or should it be seen through someone else's eyes? Then, finally, the ending — should it be the same or different, and if different, how will that affect the action that's gone on before? If, for example, the old plot has the couple walking off into the sunset happily, and we want to change it so they part sadly and go in opposite directions, then the earlier action will have to allude to that possibility through foreshadowing. Think of changes in terms of strengthening the story line, not just in terms of rearranging things to avoid legal problems.

Question: Can a story ever be plotless?

Answer: It wouldn't be a story if that were the case. We'd be writing an essay or a dissertation. Something is always going on in a story, even if it's hard to pick out. Marcel Proust wrote hundreds of pages of *Swann's Way* in stream of consciousness, and except for some recollections, there seemed little action in the story. But that was the point — the recollections *were* the story.

Question: Suppose someone offers to buy one of my plot ideas?

Answer: Take the money and run! Get his name and address, he's a live one!

Question: But people buy ideas all the time.

Answer: They buy *ideas*, not plots. An idea is what we do with a plot. For example, if we have a story about a huge fish terrorizing a seaside community, and we treat it as Peter Benchley did in *Jaws* — as a relentless search for vengeance and as a symbolic clash of good and evil — we have come up with a "treatment" of the plot. We have given life to the plot through the use of a plot motivator such as vengeance. It has become our idea, and if we want to offer this treatment for sale, it is ours to offer. That doesn't mean someone else can't have the same idea and write the story too. It does mean, though, that when our story is written, no one else can steal it completely. They can steal our plot but not our idea.

Question: Can I ever get exclusive rights to a plot so no one else will ever use it?

Answer: Our treatment of the plot is what we can copyright, and, as mentioned before, since January 1, 1978 that's protection for a period of fifty years. But if we want exclusive rights to a plot *before it is written*, we have a big job. It would be easiest if the plot concerned one person's story, and we were fortunate enough to get that person to sign an agreement giving us the exclusive rights to that story. But that wouldn't protect our story rights, if someone else involved in the story decided to tell *their* story. All we could protect are the recollections and observations of the person who signs the agreement with us. But if the plot involves a number of people, it becomes an impossible job to try and find them all and sign them up just so we can have exclusive rights. Better we take one aspect of the story, provide our own treatment and publish it before anyone else gets the same idea.

Question: What are some good sources for finding plots and stealing them?

Answer: All forms and types of literature are there for the taking, of course. As we point out in the chapters on plot motivators, the Greek legends, the Greek myths (and other cultural myths such as those from the Norse, the Hindu etc.), right up to Shakespeare and through the literature of the nineteenth and twentieth centuries are fair game. But for a shortcut, we might check our local newspaper. There's a wealth of opportunity buried in journalistic shorthand. For example, a news story about the commission of a crime or about an unusual rescue might set our creative wheels spinning. Apply "what if..." and see where it takes us. The news story, in effect, gives us the bare bones of the story. Now if we were to add a plot motivator or two and then sprinkle in a story spicer, we'd have our story line.

Question: Suppose I have a fantastic experience, and someone else wants to write about it. Can I stop them?

Answer: Here again we are asking a court to perform censorship (stopping publication before it happens). Few judges would go along with this. Our best bet is to keep our mouth shut if the other writer approaches us. He can't write about what we know if we don't tell him. Then, wait and see if anything appears in print, or ask to see a copy of the manuscript before it is published. Either way we analyze it to see if our privacy has been invaded or if we are libelled. If we think so, our next visit should be to a lawyer.

Question: What if I want to use characters from an old work — say, John Oakhurst and Mother Shipton from Bret Harte's *The Outcasts of Poker Flats?*

Answer: This story was written in 1870 and the copyright has long since run out. Use the characters — steal them. BUT — if we use them *as they appear in a revised edition* which still has copyright protection, we'd have problems. The bare plot anyone can steal at any time.

Question: Someone once told me that true-to-life details don't make a plot or a story. What do they mean?

Answer: "Just the facts... what happened?... tell it just like you saw it..." are ways of getting the details out. But they don't tell a story, they simply relate the event. Journalism tells what happened, fiction writers show us the story. For example, we witness a bank robbery. What we see are the true-to-life details, but if we dramatize the robber's motivations, describe the robbers, their victims and the police, elaborate on the tensions created by the robbery, follow the matter to a conclusion which may differ from the actual conclusion, we have a story. Writers mold stories in much the same way sculptors mold a work of art from a lump of clay. The bare facts are only the beginning for a work of fiction, and every writer will tell us... they never lift a set of circumstances out entirely. They add their own imaginings, their own sense of drama until they have molded the story.

Question: Why is motivation so important for plotting?
Answer: Readers must be convinced, they must believe that things *do* happen the way they do, and this is best accomplished by giving a "why" or a reason for such things to happen. A plot without motivation is uninteresting because the reader will constantly tell himself, "things just couldn't happen this way!" or "no one behaves this way!" A plot is a series of events connected to one another, and without motivation where's the connection?

Question: Can I quote from The Bible or use any of the stories directly without copyright or plagiarism problems?
Answer: Quoting a copyrighted version of The Bible is subject to the same limitations as quoting from any other copyrighted work. But the stories themselves are fair game, anyone can use them. (But be careful not to use someone else's "treatment" of those stories.

Question: How can I be sure an editor won't steal a plot idea from a manuscript I submit?
Answer: The simple answer is that it's unethical, if not illegal. But that doesn't mean it can't or won't happen. Anyone who has seen their name in print has had the experience of wondering about other, rejected manuscripts and whether their ideas

sparked someone else to do a story. The truth is this: editors almost never steal plot ideas — most are simply too busy with other aspects of the work. Remember, even though we may think of ourselves as the center of a small universe, there are thousands upon thousands of writers out there thinking the same thing. Is it inconceivable that two or more of us might happen upon the same idea at approximately the same time? If we have any doubts about this, pay a visit to any major magazine or book-publishing house and ask for a peek at the "slush pile" (the compilation of magazine and story ideas and manuscripts that come in unsolicited). Sometimes the pile stretches from floor to ceiling, and often there's more than one pile! Multiply this by all the publishing houses, and we get an idea that coincidence is not such a remote thing. Remember this, too: if we deal with a reputable publisher, no one in that house would think of stealing our idea. Plots can be stolen, yes, but not the way we treat a plot. A reputable editor in a reputable publishing house respects that as much as we do.

Question: When is stealing, *not* stealing and vice-versa?
Answer: When it's something every writer does, and we know it and expect it. Here's Gary Provost's attitude: "Whenever people ask me what I did for a living before I became a writer, I reply, 'I did all those crummy jobs that would some day look so glamorous on the back of a book jacket.' It's a cute line, one of many I use often in order to keep myself constantly surrounded by an aura of cleverness. But I didn't invent the line. I read it twenty years ago in a *TV Guide* article by Merle Miller, and I've used it ever since, rarely giving Miller credit for the line.

"Is that plagiarism? Have I stolen from Merle Miller? If I have, we're all in a lot of trouble, because all writers repeat cute phrases, vivid word images, clever bits of dialogue, snappy one-liners and poignant observations they have heard and read somewhere else."

Amen, we say.

Bibliography

Books

Altic, Richard D. *The Scholar Adventurers*. New York, MacMillan & Co., 1950

Altrocchi, Rudolph. *Sleuthing In the Stacks*. Cambridge: Harvard University Press, 1944.

Benet, William Rose and Pearson, Norman Holmes, editors. *The Oxford Anthology of American Literature*. New York: Oxford University Press, 1941.

Brooks, Peter. *Reading For the Plot: Design and Intention*. New York: Alfred A. Knopf, 1984.

Carpenter, Rhys. *Folk Tale Fiction and Saga in the Homeric Epics*. Berkeley: University of California Press, 1974.

Caserio, Robert L. *Plot, Story and the Novel: From Dickens and Poe to the Modern Period*. Princeton: Princeton University Press, 1979.

Chickering, Robert and Hartman, Susan. *How to Register a Copyright and Protect Your Creative Work*. New York: Scribner's, 1980.

Cook, Sir Edmund. *More Literary Recreation*. Philadelphia: R. West, 1973.

Crawford, Ted. *The Writer's Legal Guide*. New York: Hawthorn Books, 1977.

Downey, June Etta. *Creative Imagination*. New York: Harcourt Brace & Co., 1929.

Eliot, T.S. *After Strange Gods: A Primer of Modern Heresy*. New York: Harcourt Brace & Co., 1934.

Emerson, Ralph Waldo. *Quotation and Originality*. Complete Works, Vol. 8. Cambridge: Riverside Press, 1875.

Gerould, G.H. *The Patterns of English and American Fiction: A History.* New York: Russell and Russell, 1966.

Goodman, Paul. *The Structure of Literature.* Chicago: University of Chicago Press, 1954.

Grant, Michael. *The Myths of the Greeks and Romans.* New York: World Publishing, 1962.

Guthrie, W.K.C. *The Greeks and their Gods.* Boston: Beacon Press, 1968.

Judge, C.B. *Elizabethan Book Pirates.* Cambridge: Harvard University Press, 1934.

Kaplan, Benjamin. *An Unhurried View of Copyright.* New York: Columbia University Press, 1968.

Kirk, G.S. *The Nature of the Greek Myths.* Woodstock: Overlook Press, 1975.

Knowlson, T.S. *Originality: a Popular Study of the Creative Mind.* London: T.W. Laurie, 1919.

Kromer, S.N. *Mythologies of the Ancient World.* New York: Doubleday & Co., 1961.

Lindey, Alexander. *Plagiarism and Originality.* New York: Harper & Brothers, 1952

Lloyd-James, H. *The Justice of Zeus.* Berkeley: University of California Press, 1971.

Magill, Frank N. *Masterplots.* Vols 1-12, Rev. ed. Englewood Cliffs, N.J.: Salem Press, 1976.

Nicoll, Allardyce. *World Drama From Aeschylus to Anouilh.* New York: Harcourt Brace & Co., 1950.

Otto, Walter F. *The Homeric Gods.* New York: Pantheon Books, 1954.

Polti, Georges. *Thirty-Six Dramatic Situations.* Boston: Writer Inc., 1921.

Quint, David. *Origin and Originality in Renaissance Literature: Versions of the Source.* New Haven: Yale University Press, 1983.

Rose, H.J. *A Handbook of Greek Mythology.* New York: E.P. Dutton & Co., 1959.

Starrett, Vincent. *Books Alive.* New York: Random House, 1940.

Thomas, Henry. *Stories of the Great Dramas and their Authors.* New York: Garden City Publishing Co., 1939.

Thrall, William Flint and Hibbard, Addison. *Handbook to Literature,* edited by Clarence Hugh Holmon. 3rd edition, Indianapolis: Odyssey Press, 1972.

Tuchman, Barbara. *The March of Folly.* New York: Alfred A. Knopf, 1984.

White, Harold O. *Plagiarism and Imitation During the English Renaissance.* New York: Octagon Press, 1965.

Articles

Anderson, R.G. "Other Men's Thunder." *Saturday Evening Post,* January 2, 1926.

Anderson, Susan Heller. "New Novelist Is Called a Plagiarist." *New York Times,* October 21, 1980.

—"Writer Apologizes For Plagiarism." *New York Times,* October 28, 1980.

Boyer, R. "Finding a Plot For Your Novel." *Writer,* July, 1983.

Davidson, M., and Blue, M. "Writer's Guide to Copyright." *Writer,* November, 1979.

Davis, H.L. "Copyright Law: Time For Revision," *Physics Today,* September, 1982.

DeVoto, Bernard. "Always Different, Always the Same." *Saturday Review of Literature,* May 29, 1937.

Ellis, H.F. "Niceties of Plagiarism," *Atlantic Monthly,* January, 1959.

Fife, S. "Meyer Levin's Obsession," *New Republic,* August 2, 1982.

Fitzgibbon, W. "Other Men's Words," *New York Times Magazine,* February 8, 1953.

Floren, L. "Where Do You Get Your Plots?" *Writer,* May, 1958.

Ford, F. "Bugbear of Plagiarism." *The Writer,* January, 1888.

Gallico, Paul. "The Day the Real Queen Mary Nearly Turned Over at Sea: Idea for Poseidon Adventure." *Saturday Evening Post,* Fall, 1972.

Gatenby, R. "How to Devise an Ingenious Plot." *Writer,* October, 1975.

Gilbert, Henry F. "Originality." *Musical Quarterly,* January, 1919.

Gold, H. "Stories I Guess I Won't Write." *Atlantic Monthly,* August, 1969.

Greenway, J. "Honest Man's Guide to Plagiarism." *National Review,* December 21, 1979.

Hays, Arthur Garfield. "The Plagiarism Plague." *Vanity Fair,* July, 1930.

Ireland, Baron. "Plagiarism." *Harper's Magazine,* February, 1924.

Jensen, E. "Where The Action Is." *Writer's Digest,* September, 1977.

Kozak, Ellen M. "Copyright: A Guide to the 'Author's Law'." *Writer's Digest,* March, 1984.

Ladd, D. "The Future of Copyright." *Publishers Weekly,* June 1, 1984.

Levy, Newman. "They've Stolen My Plot!" *Atlantic Monthly*, July, 1949.

Peers, E., and others. "Why Writers Plagiarize." *Newsweek*, November 3, 1980.

Pollack, Channing. "The Plagiarism Racket." *American Mercury*, May, 1945.

Provost, Gary. "Do Editors Steal?" *Writer's Digest*, April, 1983.

Reed, L.F. "There's Gold In The Fine Print; Personal Columns as Basis For Stories." *Writer's Digest*, February, 1969.

Rosen, R.D. "Epping." *New Republic*, November 15, 1980.

Shaw, P. "Plagiary." *American Scholar*, Summer, 1982.

Smith, Wendy. "Martin Ais Cites Plagiarism in Jacob Epstein's Novel." *Publishers Weekly*, November 7, 1980.

Treece, J.M. "Effects of New Copyright Law," *USA Today*, August, 1978.

Unsigned. "Catching the Plagiarist." *Publishers Weekly*, November 6, 1937.

Unsigned. "Plagiarism and the Use of Factual Material: Legal Angles." *Publishers Weekly*, April 29, 1963.

Unsigned. "Self-Plagiarism." *Atlantic Monthly*, September, 1893.

Unsigned. "Suspense" (B.J. Hurwood speaks on how to devise plots for detective stories). *New Yorker*, October 3, 1983.

Vivante, A. "Plot." *Writer*, April, 1977.

Wolseley, R.E. "Who Wrote That?" *The Etude*, October, 1940.

Wrinkler, K.J. "Sweeping Revisions of the Copyright Law." *Education Digest*, January, 1977.

Zehner, H. "Plagiarism and Our Rubbery Copyright Laws." *Saturday Review*, June 24, 1978.

Index